How to Constitute a World

Eva Brann

How to Constitute a World

OUTSIDE IN, INSIDE OUT

Paul Dry Books

Philadelphia 2017

The Publisher wishes to thank Pedro J. Martinez-Fraga,
1984 graduate of St. John's College and student there of
Eva Brann, who suggested the publication of this book.

First Paul Dry Books Edition, 2017

Paul Dry Books, Inc.
Philadelphia, Pennsylvania
www.pauldrybooks.com

Printed in the United States of America

CIP data available at the Library of Congress

To the midwife's son and Diotima's pupil

CONTENTS

HOW TO CONSTITUTE A WORLD

Preface

KANT'S WRITINGS ARE the subject of the body of essays constituting this collection. He was my first philosopher. The green German edition of the *Critique of Pure Reason* (*Philosophische Bibliothek* 37a) is the most tattered book on my philosophy shelves. In a moment I'll say why—in the hope of capturing your, the reader's, good will.

The book you're holding consists of a Prelude, in which the two philosophers Heraclitus and Parmenides are juxtaposed, and of a center and bulk on some of Kant's writings, large and small. "But where is the fourth?" to quote Socrates' question that opens the dialogue *Timaeus*. We don't learn who that mysterious missing fourth is there, but here it is Plato's Socrates himself; he appears only incidentally. As Kant was the first philosopher I really *studied*, so Socrates was, long before that, the one I ardently *followed*, for five reasons. First (this mattered most in youth): He showed in the "romantic" dialogues, *Phaedrus* and *Symposium*, that thinking can be an erotic arousal of the soul. Second: Philosophizing is an activity best done in an alternation of solitary effort and human companionship. Thus the way Socrates brought philosophy down to earth is not, as Cicero claimed, by making it moral, but by making it an intra-human activity rather than a divine initiation. Third: This activity is called dialectic, conversation of a sort that sometimes pushes speech beyond its proper, that is, its logical, limits. Fourth: The way to go is through "hypothesis" (Plato, *Republic* 510 B), literally a "setting under" of an assumption that is at once *deep* and *high*. As Heraclitus says, "The way up and the way down is one and the same" (Diels-Kranz 60). Fifth: These assumptions encapsulate a faith that I think of as "philosophical optimism." What is hypothesized and then perhaps corroborated is good and desirable to know, earthly deviations notwithstanding. Plato's Socrates is the missing fourth here only because I've already written a book devoted to him, *The Music of the Republic*.

The two philosophers of the Prelude, Heraclitus and Parmenides, are usually called Pre-Socratics. Is this implicitly a denigrating denomination, as if they were purely anticipatory, *mere* preludes to the grand event? If so, it is surely a misapprehension. Socratic cautiously bold philosophizing is a falloff from the grandeur of Heraclitus' initiation by the Speech-divinity, by Logos himself, or from Parmenides' reception, perhaps by the truth-goddess Aletheia herself. Moreover, I ask myself whether, in the order of thinking ourselves into illumination, these "pre"-thinkers are mere upbeats, or seriously prior. I find it an engaging perplexity and an abidingly interesting question, perennial.

Heraclitus, chronologically the first philosopher of the West—but a late discovery for me—is a thinker of terrific depth. Socrates said of him (Diogenes Laertius II 22), that it would take a Delian diver to bring his thought to light. (The men of the island of Delos dove for sponges.) Heraclitus regards *Logos*, "Thoughtful Speech," in two ways. He is an external world-governing king who sorts things out into antagonistic kinds, which, by their mutual stresses and strains, energize a world. Then the same *Logos*, functioning immanently as *logoi*, ratios, makes these kinds mutually transformable and the stuff of the world recyclable by proportion.

Parmenides, Heraclitus' younger contemporary (early fifth century B.C.E.), discovered Being as the one and only thinkable, sayable entity: its "is-ing" is all there is. My first essay presents these two men as almost made-for-each-other opponents, by which I mean that they are antithetical but at opposite ends of the *same* spectrum. They differ in every point of execution, but they are doing the same thing; they are telling *how the world is constituted* such as to be an intelligible whole.

Thus they are both meta-physicians, thinkers who go beyond the world's obvious appearances, who penetrate and transcend them so as to dive to the true rationale or the divine truth deep *down*. Hence they are the initiators of what I might call the Western Tradition, meaning such inquiry as goes "beyond nature" (meta-physics). I say "might call" it so, were a *tradition* of inquiry not a paradox—for how can thinking be "handed over"—which is what "tradition" says and means? And yet there *is* such a tradition, a tradition-subverting tradition, which has inherited the two basic, perennially contended terms, *Logos* and *Being*, one from each of these Pre-Socratics, together with the procedure later called dialectic—the disputatious joining of minds over a common perplexity, with its occasional overleaping of the boundaries of proper, that is, logical, speech into paradox, self-contradiction, and the attendant profound perplexity which is, strangely, not a source of thwarting despair but of aroused awe.

I consider it a miracle that two men who never met should be so neatly each other's dialectical partner—a miracle I hesitate to acknowledge because, while time and temporality (the experience and its analysis) seem to me among the great *objects of* philosophizing, it also seems to me that chronology (calendrical temporality) is scarcely ever an *explanation in* philosophy. Here's an example: Add to the question "In what significant ways are the two Pre-Socratics prior to Socrates?" this even brusquer question, "Which of the two is prior in thought, the older or the younger?" You'll see that this is not a question of birth date, especially for near-contemporaries.

The five essays that constitute most of the book are about Kant, my devotion to whom has several aspects, which I'll set out here to capture, as I said, the reader's goodwill for him. (The *captatio benevolentiae* is said, in the rhetorical tradition, to be an expositor's first job.)

To begin with, I trust his probity. He poses his problems and resolves them with huge analytic power and perfect candor; there is no casuistry or subterfuge, no trickery. It is a virtue I would not especially mark in a philosopher were there not successors who shamelessly lack it. Second, a consequence of this absolute straightforwardness is that, without getting entangled in his hidden intention, a trustful reading will suddenly bring one to an unconcealed abyss: The books whose very titles say "*Critique*," meaning the setting of limits to human rational capacity, past which dogmatism ensues—are those critiques themselves well grounded? The case of most interest to me is also the most obvious: the imagination. For Kant, this capacity has an up-front and a deep-down aspect; the latter, a "hidden art," is responsible for our most crucial soul-craft: the interaction of categorizing thought with spatial-temporal sensibility. Is it adequate to consign it (be it taken as a psychological ability or ratcheted up into a critical "condition of possibility") to "the depths of the human soul" (B 181)? Such candor in the author promotes critique in the reader—and gratitude.

Third, there is—don't laugh—Kant's charm. His texts are difficult, but not more so than his world-inverting system requires. Nietzsche calls him "the great Chinese of Königsberg," by which he means, not least, certain rococo curlicues that give Kant's style a peculiar elegance (*Beyond Good and Evil* 210, 245). Learn the vocabulary, and his writings can be esthetically pleasing.

But, fourth and above all (once I had woken up to the fun and relief to be had out of finding apt characterizations for one's own time, or perhaps rather of devising a typology by which to constitute it into an epoch), I found in Kant the most radical modern, the founder of our ultimate subjectivity. The three

Critiques are world-constituting: world-reconstituting, world-inverting. Before him, the world qualified the mind; now consciousness *constitutes the world*.

In the Epilogue I go off on my own, though swept along by reading around, particularly in neuroscience, a fascinating science operating willfully in a self-confirming circle. Its basic postulate is that only sensorily confirmable evidence counts, and then the soul is set aside because there is no evidence of it! In the course of these amateur studies I discovered yet another late hero, William James, the true founder of contemporary Phenomenology, understood as the accurate description of the *phaenomena* of consciousness—another terminally honest thinker. He is, as his science requires, a "naturalist" as physicalist and a determinist as a denier of psychic spontaneity. But he says, as wisdom demands:

> Let psychology frankly admit that *for her scientific purposes* determinism may be claimed . . . [But this] assumption of psychology is merely provisional and methodological . . . The forum where [the sciences] hold discussion [about ethical matters] is called metaphysics. Metaphysics means only ["only"!] an unusually obstinate attempt to think clearly and consistently. (Abbreviated *Psychology*, 1892, Epilogue)

I offer no solution to any metaphysical problems. I have none, above all because I don't believe that metaphysics spawns "problems," meaning quandaries capable of *solution*, that is, of *dissolution*, such as make the question moot. Rather I use a figure to delineate two kinds of inquiry: into depths and into complexity—downward and outward. These are the ways of a diver and of a researcher. I declare for the currently less practiced one and admit to two postulates of my own: The first, already mentioned, says that time is (along with imagination) the central *human* mystery and as such a great object of philosophy but never its determinant: "When" has only marginal power in thinking. The second demand declares that philosophy is a faith. I intend by this postulate no extravagant know-nothingism but a kind of open-eyed sobriety acknowledging three articles: First, thinking is spontaneous, ours to summon forth but not to force into shape. Second, staying on the surface is actually less safe than diving, at least for a happy life. And third, the world, the complex beings it displays and the unifying Being it hides—Heraclitus: "Nature loves to hide" (Diels-Kranz 123)—informs our souls, while we in turn constitute it only superficially and sometimes to our detriment.

1

PRE-SOCRATICS OR
FIRST PHILOSOPHERS?

"PRE-SOCRATICS." What a peculiar appellation! A whole slew of thinkers, poetical, aphoristic, prosaic—condemned to be known as the precursors of a man who wrote nothing! Forerunners, it seems, are *ipso facto* inferior to the rightly anointed. Take John the Baptist, the canonical precursor, who says of himself, "he that cometh after me is mightier than I, whose shoes I am not worthy to bear" (Matt. 3:11). That holds not only for individuals but also for communities. Our forefathers, the writers of the *Federalist Papers*, thought of the Greek city states, the *poleis*, whose frame or *politeia* was a direct democracy, as the unstable antecedents of the reliable representative republic they were proposing for America—not that the Greek democracies did not have some representational fea-

The author delivered this lecture as the keynote address at the annual meeting of the Metaphysical Society of America in Annapolis, Maryland, in March 2016, the theme of which was "Thinking with the Pre-Socratics."

tures, but as James Madison, remarkably, puts it: "The true distinction between these and the American Government *lies in the total exclusion of the people in their collective capacity from any share in the latter*" (*Federalist* 63; italics mine). So the superiority of our successor republic lies in erasing direct popular participation altogether—and here is my presumption: Just as the founders, as successors to the Greeks, had a deeper understanding than the latter did of the chief, philosophically opaque, element of modern politics—namely, representationalism—so John the Baptist, as forerunner of Christ, lacked his revelatory power: John baptizes with water, but Jesus will baptize with the Holy Ghost; what John is doing is significant but opaquely primitive.

Thus as "pre-somebodies" the Pre-Socratics may be thought of as deficient, lacking something, primitive in the derogatory sense. Of course, there is the opposite perspective: These men were not primitive or without sophistication, but primeval, deeper, more receptive to origins, to everything—for which the Germans have that awe-bestowing prefix *ur*, as in *Ursprung*, the "original leap." I am thinking of Heidegger, for whom what professional philosophers like to regard as progress is, in fact, a progressive occultation and a withdrawal of Being.

What did the man who devised the designation actually mean? In 1815, in an address titled "On the Worth of Socrates as a Philosopher," Friedrich Schleiermacher, the philosopher-theologian (and superb translator of Plato), declared that Socrates was pivotal in the history of philosophy. His reason seems a little underwhelming: Before Socrates there were different schools of philosophy pursuing different kinds of philosophy; after him, although the kinds were still distinguished, every school cultivated all kinds. Thus Schleiermacher kindly credits Socrates with preventing an incipient academic specialization. This view must have seemed plausible, because Schleiermacher's label "Pre-Socratic" stuck and is now used without further comment for collections of texts.

The notion that Socrates was epochal, not as the human phenomenon of the Platonic dramas, but as a historical event, appears in the first history of philosophy, Books I and II of Aristotle's *Physics*, and again in Book I of his *Metaphysics*. The latter presents Socrates as "busying himself with moral matters and not at all with the Whole of nature [as did the preceding so-called "physicists"], however seeking in those matters the universal, and being first to fix his thinking on definitions" (I.6)—a far more epochal distinction than Schleiermacher's. Here, too, he calls those who became "the Pre-Socratics" the "first wise men" (I.5). This description strikes me as significant in two ways: First, it implies that they were not "lovers" of— here meaning *"not* in secure possession of"—wisdom, but that they were *actually* wise, which delineates accurately the prevailing one of the two modes I will single out in a moment. Second, it raises a question. In calling them the "first wise men," does Aristotle mean "earliest," or is there a hint that they studied "first things" and were concerned with what he calls "the first [science]" or "first philosophy" (VI.1)?

Let me inject myself here into this epoch-framing debate. Let's give up "Pre-Socratics" and call these folks "Pre-Professionals" and their successors "Post-Socratics," with Socrates as pivot between them. That would relocate the disparagement away from the "wise men" to the professionals, where Heidegger, at least, might agree it belongs.

That isn't going to happen, however, because nothing is stickier than historical epoch terms. Take, for example, our grandest epoch-division, with which I grew up: B.C. and A.D., "Before Christ" and "In the year of our Lord," *Anno Domini*. In our era of offense-taking, some folks couldn't bear to live in the epoch of a young Jewish rabbi, so now we write B.C.E., "Before the Common Era," and C.E., "Common Era." But the turning point is still the birth date of Joshua or Jesus of Galilee, whenever that actually was, except we've masked that fact. Concerning Socrates as an epochal figure, I have my own take on the respect in which he is indeed a pivot: It is he who turns the wisdom (*sophia*) of the divinely initiated into the longing for wisdom (*philo-sophia*) of a mere mortal left to his own devices, so that Pre-Socratic truth passes into Socratic inquiry; past this inflection, this cusp, which is the human singularity called Socrates, his hypothetically held thoughts stiffen into doctrines maintained by schools.

Now back to the Pre-Socratic epoch of philosophy. Aristotle, as I said, the first practitioner of history of philosophy—perhaps as rousingly mystifying a notion *about* philosophy as ever arises *within* it—refers to an early school he calls, as I said, the "physicists" (*physikoi*) or the "accountgivers of *physis* (*physiologoi*)," among whom he places all the Pre-Socratics, including Heraclitus (III.5), but evidently not Parmenides (I.2), both of whom were certainly older than Socrates. These so-called physicists were surely philosophers—as Aristotle says of them, they were "the ones who philosophized first" (*Metaphysics* I.3). And they were not crude materialists, mere believers in stuff, in matter. They "thought that the principle of all things was in certain kinds of material," which changed the qualities of matters while persisting beneath them. So when I translate Aristotle's term for the physicists' focus, *hyle*, as "material" and not as "matter," I mean that they thought of the underlying principle—be it water, air, earth, or fire—not as sensory stuff experienced by its own qualities, but as bestowing sensible moistness, lightness, lumpishness on the distinct matters that constitute nature in one of its aspects. To these they added agencies of continuous or periodic change, somewhat imaginatively or (if you will) mythically conceived, such as Love-and-Strife.

When Aristotle calls these deep inquirers into the principles of the palpable world "physicists," he implies, I imagine, that they are not yet what I might call "meta-physicists." They give an account of *physis* in terms which yet belong to the sensed world; they ground nature in its own terms. (The Pythagoreans are, perhaps, an early exception; their principles are numbers and ratios, though these appear sensorily.)

The title of Aristotle's *Metaphysics*, the greatest book in its line, is explained in two ways. First, mundanely: the composition that came "after," *meta*, the *Physics*. And second, more thoughtfully: The composition called the *Metaphysics* follows the one called the *Physics* (a plural in English as in Greek) because the many-faceted inquiry called "physics," the search for the notions explaining bodies undergoing change, precedes "metaphysics," the singular inquiry into the principles "beyond" (*meta*) those reached in the book on moving beings, the *Physics*. The *Physics* ends with a logic-driven proof that if the inquiry into moving bodies is to find a resting place, then there must be a true principle of motion, a real beginning, which must be such that it can move others without itself being in want of an explanation of its motion—that is, an unmoved mover. The *Metaphysics* is the subsequent inquiry, which develops the terms that can be used to transcend physics and delineate an unmoving but movement-causing divinity: *Nous*, the god who is mind, an unloving beloved, the aboriginal unmoved mover, the self-sufficient "self-thinking" being, Thought of Thought (*noesis noeseos*).

For the rest of this essay, I want to excise the physiologues who, though on the brink of this step beyond, and thus philosophers, are still not quite metaphysicians—except for the two, Heraclitus and Parmenides. By generation, they certainly belong to the first philosophers, but I will claim that they are also first philosophers in Aristotle's sense of "First Philosophy": the knowledge of the ultimate individual being (*ousia*), if there is one, and of Being (*to on*) as Being (*Metaphysics* VI.1)—its ever pursued and ever perplexing subject (VII.1). *"First" philosophers they are—but not quite.*

Heraclitus, the first of the first, needs more defense in this respect than Parmenides. Aristotle counts him among the physicists because he makes fire a first principle. It is a misunderstanding: Heraclitus does indeed bring in a physical fire, an analytic agent, so to speak, of matter. But his primary fire is identical with his world principle, the Logos. This fiery Logos is both a discerning, dividing, *analytic* cosmic ruler *and* an intraworld *arche* or *ruling* beginning. *Arche* is usually translated as "principle," literally "what seizes first place." Heraclitus is far more wonderful than that; the Logos-Fire is not a mere cosmic captain.

While I'm at it, let me relieve him of a silly but tightly attached epithet, the "Philosopher of Flux," who is said to have said that "All is flux" (*panta rhei*, "everything flows"; nothing stays)—a notion which no person of his taut ingenuity, which made him the first discoverer of physical transformations tightly controlled by numerical ratios, could have perpetrated. (I'll come back to those ratios, *logoi* in Greek.) As for "Everything flows," he never said it. Plato reports that "those around him" attributed to him the notion that all things are in flux, and he has Socrates add "like leaky pots" (*Cratylus* 440 c.). I will add this: Beware of Heracliteans, the Heraclitus-followers; they make willful mincemeat of him, including the propagation of his obscurity, "Heraclitus the Obscure." He isn't obscure; he says deep things concisely. But he isn't disciple-friendly, congenial, sociable—the pre-schooler of philosophy, you might say.

Heraclitus is generally believed to be slightly Parmenides' elder, perhaps by a short generation, a quarter-century. (A generation that puts fewer than thirty years between the birth of the father and the son is sometimes called a "short generation" by chronologists.) But though close in time, they lived apart in place. Heraclitus, the one generally thought of as the philosopher of flux, was entirely sessile as far as we know, living all his life among his despised Ephesians. On the other hand, Parmenides of Elea, the defender of motionlessness, traveled as far as Athens, where he got into a chronologically difficult, but intellectually entirely feasible, conversation with young Socrates (Plato, *Parmenides*).

I want to interject myself here again: I had the good fortune to find myself on the site of his beloved city, Elea, where he functioned as statesman. I can tell you, I was suddenly seized with awe, because here the most astounding thought of all occurred to a human being capable of giving it utterance—that of all-pervasive Being.

Nevertheless, neither place nor time seems to me of the least consequence to my project for the rest of this essay. I intend to put Heraclitus and Parmenides into conversation with each other, and in doing so to transmute a problem in the empirical history of philosophy—meaning an only circumstantially insoluble puzzle—into a reflective question within philosophy itself—meaning an abiding perplexity stemming from the nature of things. That genuine question is: Which philosopher is truly first? More precisely: What is first, Logos or Being? Or is that perhaps not the best way to put the question? Should it perhaps be: Are the two Founding Fathers talking about different things in somewhat the same way or about the same thing in different ways; or—may the god Apollo help us—about different things in different ways?

Let me right now exclude the last of these. If it were actually possible, then the history of philosophy would be as insignificant as the dated list of English kings which their young subjects used to be driven to learn by heart. For what animates philosophy's history is that it is dialectical, that is to say, conversationally antithetical: It moves in oppositions that are congenial enough to be heard and taken up in responsive talk. I think it can be shown that these first two, Heraclitus and Parmenides, were—and I don't know how else to put it—*providentially* fraternal in their opposition. Sometimes the heavens don't wait for historians to bestow meaning on what is usually a mere mess of happenstance, but actually arrange for significance to eventuate.

What then are these two speaking about that is the same—one writing appropriately in aphorisms, the other fittingly in hexameters?

They both speak of *the All*. Heraclitus, as we would expect, *always* says it in the plural: *panta*, "all things" (in fourteen relevant places). Parmenides almost always uses the singular, *pan*, "everything" (D.-K. 8; citations are to the fragment numbers in Diels-Kranz, *Die Fragmente der Vorsokratiker*; ["D.-K." is omitted hereafter].). This ambition to comprehend the whole of what there is—not from within as a sensing being among sensible things, but from without, as an apprehending intelligence that can reach beyond the sensed world—puts these two squarely among the "transcenders," among Aristotle's metaphysicians.

They bear themselves, however, not as lovers of a wisdom to be pursued, that is, as philosophers, but as knowers of a wisdom that has been imparted to them. Both speak as initiates, Heraclitus in an oracular style rivaling that of Apollo's temple in Delphi (93), Parmenides as an initiate, outdoing Homer, the poet-pupil of the Olympian Muses, who could not claim to have reached the inner heart of truth in a piping chariot, as did the philosopher-poet (1).

What is the frame of mind of a human being who is the first in his world to utter: "all things" or "everything"? It is scarcely possible to recapture the wonder of it for the speaker who has so leaped beyond the world that is home, to imagine his sense of being set apart from the rest of humanity, which sees from within and not from beyond. Evolutionists are committed to the notion that intelligence developed in a continuum, in tiny increments. Yet insight does not seem to arrive that way, but rather in a life-altering jolt: the world-principle speaks to a solitary who can hear, or a youth's chariot bursts through the welcoming gates of the House of Truth—and their thinking veers into new ways.

The *Logos*, Speech itself, speaks to solitary Heraclitus and bids him see and hear and feel in what way "all things" cohere. *Aletheia*, Truth itself, speaks to Parmenides, the future statesman, and orders him to forgo all speech but the one word that conveys the way in which everything "is" seamlessly one.

The Logos tells Heraclitus that it—perhaps I should say "he," for it is a god we're speaking of (32)—Speech himself, discriminates *and* collects all things just as his subordinate words, his *logoi*, do. They *distinguish* all things by different names, proper names, and they *gather* all things under the same name,

"Gathering," for behind the word *logos* stands the verb *legein*, whose first meaning is "to gather" and only then "to speak."

Truth tells Parmenides the one and only word that tells the truth: "Is," *esti*. Greek syntax permits *esti* to be a complete sentence, one word that comprehends the whole. There is no personal pronoun to divide "is" from itself, to make us ask, "*What is?*" *Is-ing* is. All "not-is" is not to be spoken, and the diversity it spawns not to be regarded, says Parmenides' Truth, while Heraclitus' Logos enjoins both listening to his utterance *and* looking into the teeming *Cosmos* (89). Truth demands silence and withdrawal into *Being*. (Parmenides also enters a second way, the "Way of Seeming [*doxa*]," which yields a fanciful cosmogony. I used to be in some perplexity about why he spoiled his single-minded grandeur by taking the previously proscribed way of the "double-pated" folk [*dikranoi*, 6], who dither distractedly. Then I read Heidegger's *Introduction to Metaphysics* [1935], in which he asserts that even Parmenides' solidly homogeneous Being *requires* a complementary "restriction" by Seeming [74 ff.]. Now I'm in total perplexity: Isn't that a nullifying intrusion into the unbreachable uniformity of Being that is Parmenides' great insight?)

At this point let me recollect what I've laid out so far and make clear where I'm going. These two have in common the thought of a whole. This is a spectacularly new thought: the notion that the Whole is to be comprehended in its Wholeness, the idea that Wholeness comes from outside the Whole, is imparted from beyond. It is, as I would put it, a logical necessity that wholeness should elicit the following duality: A whole might be a "one-over-many," a captained collection, an embattled unity of co-existences. Or it might be a "one-is-one," and all alone, a fused unity devoid of inner discrimination. The third case, a whole of total multiplicity, is not thinkable, like the "all is flux" falsely attributed to Heraclitus. If there is only multitude, sheer diversity, then there is no whole and nothing to transcend, since such a flux is subject neither to an inner organization nor to an outer delimitation. If there were limits, somewhere the fluxing would have to cease, double back on itself, develop vortices or whatever—some structure.

For all their primeval grandeur, Heraclitus and Parmenides were human, and so had temperaments. Perhaps some context of their lives, respectively in Asia Minor and in Western Italy had some effect on their thinking—who knows? In any case, Heraclitus chose to stay put and to behold the world as a heterogeneous collection, while Parmenides decided to travel and to view the world as a homogenized unity. Having claimed that their first concern was the same, the Whole, I would now like to show how they lay out these wholes in what I'll call "antithetical complements." I mean that they don't talk *past* each other but—almost—responsively, *to* each other. They don't, however, argue; they *announce*.

One more preliminary: To do these Pre-Socratics justice as being, both of them, "ontologists," devotees of Being, I think it is necessary to *believe what you see* in the transmitted texts. For example, when Heraclitus utters paradoxes such as this one— the cosmic wisdom *does* and *does not* want to be called by the name of "Zeus" (32)—we must not set it aside as high-handed obscurantism but receive it as an exact enunciation of a significant thought. The Logos both appears and withdraws as a godhead: appears so when the initiate is in a mood of worship, withdraws when he is in the mode of thinking. When Parmenides says that "to be and to think is the same" (3), we must accept it as a remarkable possibility instead of diddling the text into saying something flabby such as, "The same thing is there for thinking and being." Both of these apostasies are committed by willful scholars. Yet, in dealing with these early wise men, "having it your way" is the same as "not getting it."

So now to some specific comparisons, five particularly responsive appositions, some of which I have already broached. Take them, if you will, as testimonials to what seems to me, once again, to be one of the few truths revealed by time: The Western philosophical tradition is "dialectical," I mean self-opposing, from its very inception—and ever after, even when dialectic becomes quibbling. Heraclitus (b. circa 540 B.C.E.) always comes first, because he is usually regarded, as I've said, as being Parmenides' (b. circa 515) elder by a short generation.

So then, *One:* Heraclitus exhorts us to listen to Speech Itself, to the Logos Himself, and to "say the same," *homologein*, as says the Logos about his cosmic "collecting," to agree with him. (Again, I say "his," because this Logos is Heraclitus' divinity.) The actual word for "collect," *syllegein*, is not voiced but is, I think, to be heard by the hearing listener (50). Parmenides, on the other hand, is effectively consigned to silence by the goddess, Truth Herself, when she proscribes negation and predication (8). The fact that the goddess herself speaks and uses negation is an overt self-contradiction that presages the downfall of this grandest of all thoughts (Plato, *Sophist* 237 ff.). Heraclitus' paradoxes *speak* his mind while Parmenides' contradictions *refute* his. As their enjoined missions differ, so do their means. Heraclitus speaks in pithy paradoxical prose, often framed as "nominal" or "gnomic" sentences, meaning sentences that lack the copula "is," and speak verbless, that is, timeless wisdom, for example, *hen : panta*, "everything [is] one" (50). For Parmenides this copula-word, *esti*, becomes, all by itself, a sentence; it is *the* positive proposition of his teaching (2), which is delivered in epic hexameters. The stylistic contrast mirrors their characters. Heraclitus is, as I've said, a sessile solitary, a curmudgeonly despiser of his unreceptive fellow-citizens (21), who speaks to them sparely and brusquely of cosmic truths and who devises his own aphoristic prose; Parmenides is a well-loved statesman in his city and a traveler in Greece, who goes to Athens, where he instructs an eager young Socrates in dialectic (Plato, *Parmenides*), and who sings his teaching in Homeric resonances.

Two: The basic terms of their language (as distinct from their style) also attest their antithetical fraternity. As I said, Heraclitus always speaks severally of *"panta,"* "all things," "everything" (8, 10, 50). Parmenides always speaks jointly of *"pan,"* "all, the whole" (8). The antithesis itself lies in this: For Heraclitus the constituents of "everything" are alternately locked in mutually supported stasis, in inimical stability, hostile reliance, like stand-up wrestlers who butt at and abut on each other in a temporary hold (51), and then again are pulled apart by the referee, here the Logos. Thus the collection of striving elements is transformed, not chaotically, but according to precise *mathematical ratios*, called *logoi* in Greek, the plural of *logos*. These ratios are the mini-agents of the Logos at work in the world; they supervise transformations of matter obeying the dictates of a very modern chemical law: the law fixing the ratios of masses in the transformation of substances; for instance, so much of water into so much of earth, in every case of transformation (31). This Heraclitean cosmos is simultaneously positive and negative, discontinuous and unbounded, with a ruling Logos who at once governs from beyond the collection and is actively immanent (4, 108). Such a world is twice oppositional: Each being opposes its other individually, and all elements collectively dissolve and supersede one another; there is strife and stability, decomposition and reconstitution.

Parmenides' "whole" is internally *without differentiation* and so without negation, qualification, change, or locomotion—a perfect, impenetrable, well-balanced sphere, continuous and contained, homogeneous and bounded (8). This impenetrability of Being to otherness is also its translucence to itself, as thought is penetrable to thought—for Being *is* Thought (3). Parmenides never asks about the features of its surround, since all that *is*, is within. Nor does he ask about the name of its location, since that would have to be the *Is-not*, the Nothing, the very term and thought he has forsworn. I might remind the reader here that Heidegger will, as it were, supplement Parmenides in his essay "What is Metaphysics?" (1929). He surrounds the region of beings and Being with "The Nothing" for which Dasein is the "place-holder" amid worldly beings, having been pulled into the Nothing by means of an ontological feeling called "anxiety," thence to view beings as a whole.

Three: Heraclitus' cosmos is a rational, that is, ratio-governed, collection of numerically related elementary stuff; the bodies shaped from it are in relations of *tension*, which is a force governing matter that is at once attractive and repulsive and *everywhere the same* in the tension-effecting connection, say a bow-string (51).

Parmenides' world is, on the contrary, *a thought*, as I've just mentioned. He says unequivocally: "For it is the same to think and to be"—*to gar auto noein esti te kai einai* (3, and he says it again at 8). That's the text, which Plotinus, with his Pre-Socratic empathy, translates just as I have (*Enneads* V.1). I've already mentioned that some scholars can't believe their eyes: Parmenides, in the early fifth century B.C.E., speaking like a German idealist—Fichte, Schelling—of the early nineteenth century C.E.! To me it makes sense. Utter simplicity is the inception of idealism. The ratifying text here is Plato's *Parmenides*, in which Parmenides seems to have traveled to Athens just to demonstrate in young Socrates' presence that the contradicting kind of conversation called *dialectic* is potent and necessary training for formulating perplexities but that it is *perfectly impotent* and even stymieing in attaining ultimate insight. For example, in order to settle the Heraclitean-Parmenidean question "Many or One?"—which is also, not accidentally, the central issue of Plato's dialogue—thought must outstrip speech. Thus, incidentally and cunningly, Parmenides secures his goddess's silence as ultimate. Dialectic must go silent within sight of Truth, as Plato emphasizes in his *Seventh Letter* (341c ff.).

Four: These antithetical brothers share the root of irreconcilability: extremism, but in opposing directions. Heraclitus is, to my mind, *sui generis*, one of a kind, never repeated among his successors, even those who quote him. Plato makes Eryximachus, the physician-banqueter of the *Symposium* (his name means "Belchbattler"; he cures Aristophanes' hiccups), draft Heraclitus into the service of harmonizing Love (187a). Nietzsche finds him—ludicrously—comforting (*Ecce Homo*, 3). Even Schopenhauer, closest to Heraclitus in advancing strife as a world-principle—though, to be sure, farthest away in the ultimate pessimism of his world-mood—ends by looking for an escape from conflict in disinterested esthetic contemplation and renunciation of the trouble-making will (*The World as Will and Representation*, Bk. VI). Heidegger, who understands Heraclitus' cosmic war as both world-generating and world-preserving, attributes to him not, indeed, an ultimate, but an originary unity, a "collectedness of Being" (*Introduction to Metaphysics*, 47, 130)—which is contradicted in a fragment that says, "Out of all things one, and out of one all things" (10)—turn by turn: all things collected into a unity and the unity dispersed into all things.

Those mitigators are the Post-Socratics. Not so, never so, Heraclitus. He finds kingliness in war (*polemos*, 53), justice in strife (80), advantage in abrasiveness (8), and truth-telling in self-contradiction. He even censures Homer for praying that battle might disappear among gods and among men. I might inject now that Heraclitus seems to me, in his feel for his tensely muscular cosmos and his adoption of a brusquely handsome language, closest of all to Hobbes—though Hobbes is, most peremptorily, no metaphysician, but both a materialist and a mechanist, while Heraclitus' discerning Logos is both a metaphysical principle and an immanent operator. Under him, stress and strain is thus ultimate, neither in fact nor in wish resolvable; when the antagonists come apart, when their enlivening *agon* and their invigorating agony ceases, it is only to mark a world-transformation and a new polemical array. There is, in my reading, nothing else like this in ontology—this ultimate clash of *joyfully irreconcilable*, vividly assertive beings, held in their controlled confrontation by the World-speaker, a Referee, the divine Logos himself: articulate thinking in the service of a pervasively tensed cosmos.

Parmenides' holism too is never again equaled in the Western ontological tradition, as far as I know—though perhaps it has its negative counterpart in the Nirvana of the East. His Being commands total submersion and ultimate silence. These are not conditions much to the taste of actively thinking human beings, and so, in Plato's greatest ontological dialogue, the *Soph-*

ist (241d), a sort of "parricide" is committed. Father Parmenides is dialectically killed so that the Unity of Being may be penetrated by Otherness, diversity of kinds established, gradations of beings grounded, speaking and its negations recovered, and the capacity to tell truths and falsehoods regained and with it the ability to distinguish thoughtful human beings from pretenders, philosophers from sophists.

So much for their shared extremism at opposite ends of the ontological spectrum, Heraclitus at the remote end of terminal discord, Parmenides at the far terminus of ultimate union.

Five: In my title, "Pre-Socratics or First Philosophers?" I suggest that these two men might have been philosophers. Well, I must now draw back, as I've already intimated, and say instead that they were actually pre-philosophers. For though the word "philosophy" is said to have been coined by Pythagoras for his attachment to his arithmetical principles (D.-K. I 454, 35), I think of philosophy in the Socratic sense: wisdom loved, as distinct from wisdom possessed. Heraclitus himself, a younger man than the Pythagoras he despised, uses the word—he often borrows where he denigrates (40)—as an adjective. He says, "Wisdom-loving (*philosophous*, 35) men must inquire into a pretty large lot of things." (For "inquire" he uses the verb of the term *historia* with which Herodotus starts his *History*.) That seeking of information, now called "research," is not, at least to Socrates, the way of philosophy, which goes inward by way of recollection to recover congenital knowledge rather than outward in a roving search to find facts. Heraclitus doesn't even use "wise," *sophos*, when speaking of human capacities (118); his words are *phronesis* and *nous*, discretion and intelligence—for him gifts of discrimination, befitting the Logos and his manifold cosmos.

Parmenides doesn't speak of wise men or wisdom-loving at all, but rather he calls himself "the man who knows" (*eidota phota*, 1), whom Truth has chosen "to find out all things" (*panta pythesthai*, 1). The others are "double-pated know-nothings" (*dikranoi, eidotes ouden*) who think, indiscriminately, that "ever-to-be and not to be" are the same—or just that "nothing is" (6).

Heraclitus and Parmenides are both men who think of themselves as *in the know*, not conceitedly as self-sufficient discoverers, but proudly, as recipients of gifts from their respective divinities. Yet *what* they know is nearly antithetical: The Whole is Many / The Whole is One.

I'll conclude first with an observation about these great Greeks—but perhaps not only them. It could be that many thinking Greeks and their successors adopted this mode because it suited both their dispositions and their experiences, the mode namely of complementary antithesis, of reciprocally necessary opposition. The Latinate languages help; for example, *ob-ponere* and *cum-ponere*, "to oppose" and "to compose," to confront and to reconcile, are etymologically and semantically abutting notions. A prime philosophical product of this way of seeing the world is the old Pythagorean Table of Opposites (Aristotle, *Metaphysics* I.5), among whose pairs are *One/Many* and *Men/Women*. An even earlier example, a poetic case of such complementing opposition, is presented by the *Iliad* and the *Odyssey*, each of which is the other's specific other: short-lived Achilles/long-lived Odysseus, confining camps/rovable seas, warring males/seductive demigoddesses, stark reality/vivid fantasy. Or, in the hybrid realm of fictional hero and real-life initiate, we find the elderly hero Odysseus "of many turns," who has sailed all over the sea and has known the towns of many men, and the young, inexperienced sage-to-be, Parmenides, who drives his chariot overland, straight into the heart of a single truth; both tell of their journeys to realms beyond in epic hexameter.

So Heraclitus and Parmenides embody the oppositional mode—as it were, providentially—at the very beginning of articulate thinking and published thought. Heraclitus is the teller of Manyness, of ultimately unresolvable, paradoxically unifying antagonisms, Parmenides the voice of Oneness, of primordially unbreachable, speech-defying, seamless unity.

This might, next, be a good moment to ask an intriguing but essentially idle question: Why does the proponent of multiplicity precede the adherent of unity chronologically, even if it is by a little? Let me try a conjecture. I'm persuaded that thinking and speaking can *occur* separately—people can think without speaking and speak without thinking—but all I've read tells me that they *develop* conjointly. "Infants," meaning "speechless" babies who soon after birth can see pretty perfectly, who can distinguish depths, discern bodies, notice identities, are still "non-speakers" and probably only potentially thinkers, "not-yet-thinkers." In other words, the discernment of the senses precedes the reflection of the intellect: seeing precedes listening. Perhaps philosophy recapitulates ontogeny, and our tradition of inquiry into Being tracks our development as human beings. We can *see* and *distinguish* the Manyness before we can *think* and *say* its Oneness. Who knows?!

Were these two fathers superseded by their progeny? Were they left behind in the progress of thinking, in the course of which seers turned, via one true amateur, Socrates, into professionals and revealed wisdom pivoted, by way of question-asking, into problem-solving? Were they voices crying in an uncultivated wilderness, foretelling the anointed proficients? Were they primitive beginners—or never-again-equaled originators?

Hegel and Nietzsche had deep respect for them as forerunners; Heidegger, more radically, regards them as the bearers of Being, the only true preoccupation of our existence, whose illuminations were dispersed and vaporized by subsequent professors of philosophy. Their wisdom is to be brought back in an act of re-petition (*Wieder-holung*), which is accomplished by the "destruction" (*Destruktion*) or, in the accepted mitigating translation, the "deconstruction" of the ontological tradition between us and them (*Being and Time*, §6).

To me, Socrates, the pivot-point between the few Pre-Socratics and all the subsequent philosophers, seems to be the incarnate answer to this Heideggerian extremism. The first philosophers speak awe-inspiring but riddling truths, which demand mulling over and questioning—enough for two-and-a-half millennia and then some. Their own *natural* awe, which still elicits ours, is earliest. The latest is Heidegger's explicitly *willful*, that is, forcibly disruptive, questioning and his insistence that philosophical questioning is about "extra-ordinary things" and is done by extra-ordinary people (*Introduction to Metaphysics*, pp. 16, 10, 133), by rare "authentic" existences impelled by ontological anxiety.

Between awe and anxious aggression stands Socratic question-asking in its modestly receptive, ironically knowing, faith-borne openness. That, to me, makes him the game-changing pivot-point, and rightly the name-bestowing epoch-maker. Though deeply indebted to both Heraclitus and Parmenides, he serves, in the Platonic dialogues, particularly in the *Sophist*, as the instigator of equally deep inquiry into these Pre-Socratics' great terms: Logos, Being, Nonbeing. And he also—critically—anticipates his latest and, for the time being, last successor, Heidegger, in respect to questions and instigations. For Socratic questions are not driven by will but drawn by love (*Symposium* 204e, *Phaedrus* 234c; both play on the homonymic features in Greek of "love" [*eros*, gen. *erotos*] and "question" [*erotesis*]). His occasions are not the extraordinary but the ordinary, and his philosophizing is carried on in that self-confidently self-deprecating mode called *eironeia* in Greek, for which the translation "irony" is not quite adequate; it means a dissembling modesty that claims ignorance but intimates knowledge. This Socratic irony, it seems to me, is the *precise* counterpart to a question. For a question also claims ignorance—else, why would it be asked?—and intimates knowledge—else, how could it recognize its answer? (*Meno* 80d).

Let me finish by putting the same thought in a different way. Why does Socrates appear between "Pre-" and "Post-"? Why is he a hinge, a cusp, a point-of-inflexion between primeval awe and anxious willing? To be sure, it is a very asymmetric "pre" and "post"—half a century before, two-and-a-half millennia after. Nonetheless, the nineteenth-century name for these Pre-Socratics does put him at the center and declares him a turning point. Why, really? Because he turns wisdom into the love of wisdom (*sophia/philosophia*) by *putting a question mark to reverent awe*; awe with a question mark is "wonder" (*thauma*), and as he says, "This passion especially belongs to the philosopher—wondering; for there is no other origin of philosophy than this" (*Theaetetus* 155d). I think that Socrates is epochal because he undergirds truth-seeking with the motive-feeling of wonder, which is not an excludingly arcane anxiety, but an inclusively ordinary capacity—that for a non-rapacious arousal of interest. From that vantage point, the question of my title can be answered like this: If the wonder-inciting knowledge of his own ignorance be the philosopher's mark, then Heraclitus and Parmenides, the initiates, were *pre*-philosophers, Pre-Socratics, not yet knowing ignorance.

But if they did come within hearing and within sight of what is now and ever will be the concern of philosophy, namely, telling Speech and stable Truth, and if they confidently announced what the one heard and the other saw, they were indeed doubly first—the *first* to engage in *First* Philosophy and to launch it with their antithetical first principles: an active, discerning, world-governing Logos and a steadfast, translucent, world-constituting Being.

2

AN APPRECIATION OF KANT'S
CRITIQUE OF PURE REASON

AN INTRODUCTION FOR STUDENTS

T HE *CRITIQUE OF PURE REASON* runs to 884 pages in its final
form. Of these the last five are devoted to a history of metaphysics. Here Kant casts an eye over all the efforts preceding
his own and sees them as structures in ruins (B 880).[1] Then he
closes with these words:

> The critical way alone is still open. If the reader has been
> obliging and patient enough to wander over it in my com-
> pany, he may now judge whether, if he is willing to con-

This essay was first published in *Essays in Honor of Jacob Klein*, ed. Samuel S. Kut-
ler (St. John's College Press, 1976).

[1] A and B indicate the first and second editions respectively (1781 and 1786). P
stands for *Prolegomena to Any Future Metaphysics*. Other texts are cited by paragraph whenever possible. Italics are the author's throughout.

tribute his part in order to make this foot-path a royal road, something which many centuries have been unable to accomplish may not be attained *before the completion of the present century*: namely, that human reason shall, in those matters which have at all times, though before this in vain, engaged its desire to know, be given *complete satisfaction*.

The year is 1787.

I have quoted this last paragraph to establish the full *tremendousness* of this book. It means revolution, more swift, radical, and complete than the two great political revolutions in France and America between which it falls. Kant himself emphasizes this revolutionary character by taking as his paradigm the Copernican Revolution, that jolting change of point of view which turns the human being from a quietly central spectator of the moving heavens into a circulating observer who sees in nature only his own restlessness (B xvi, xxiii, n.). I shall try in this presentation to work out as exactly as possible the effect of an acceptance of this reversal on our understanding of our own humanity. But to succeed it will be necessary to strip the *Critique* of those defensive outworks which, while intended to make the newly established position secure as *the* position of liberation, in effect turn it into a new orthodoxy. For like all radical positions, the *Critique* is meant to be completely and irresistibly compelling. That is to say, those who yield to its compulsion and join, so to speak, the party, must come to see their position as obvious, final, and in no way wonderful. This lack of wonder is just what Kant aims at when he says that within the next two decades human reason shall have its desire to know completely satisfied.

The compulsion of the *Critique* is expressed by Kant in the sentence: "The *critical* way alone is still open." Therefore, if we want to remain open to the impact of the book, we must refuse to be herded along this road, though we must follow it at our own pace. We shall try to look at the *Critique* not "critically," that is, as insiders, but *appreciatively*, as outsiders. This has one immediate consequence for our reading of the text. Those compelled to live within the system must adjust it constantly to make it viable, but an outsider can afford to take it in its integrity. I shall, therefore, accept Kant's clear statements to the effect that his system was in every part complete in the first edition of 1781, that he made no change or addition when he revised the text for the second edition, and that he desired none to be made subsequently (B xxxviii).

To avoid the compulsion of the "critical way" we must see what it is. There is one best way to do that, which is to regard the *Critique*, as Kant himself does, as a great dwelling, an architectural work (B 736), erected on the ruins of preceding structures, through which we allow ourselves to be led as prospective inhabitants, attentive and yet preserving our inner independence. Let me illustrate what I mean by simply launching into a brief, and, I hope, liberating, tour of the *Critique*. The first part of this presentation will, then, deal with the critical enterprise as a whole, under three headings: the *Problems*, the *Critique*, the *System*.

Part I. The Critical Enterprise
    a. The Problems
    b. The Critique
    c. The System
Part II. The Critical Man
    a. The Subject
    b. The Predicate
    c. The Object
    d. Experience
    e. Meaning

PART I. THE CRITICAL ENTERPRISE

a. The Problems

The outworks and forecourts of the *Critique* are the problems through which Kant compels everyone to enter his book. Let me first read them off:

How is pure mathematics possible?
How is pure natural science possible?
How is metaphysics possible? (B 20 ff.)

And finally, the translation into Kant's technical language of these three together:

How are *a priori* synthetic judgments possible? (B 19)

The first three questions express Kant's two main preoccupations for many years before the critical answer came to him, namely the value and trustworthiness of Newton's mathematical science of moving bodies on the one hand, and the self-contradictoriness and uncertainty of metaphysics on the other. Yet they constitute not so much the opening of an inquiry as the gates to the straight and narrow path of a solution. If we are not to become the unwitting captives of Kant's castle, we must become thoroughly aware of the constraints which the formulations of these problems impose on our way.

First of all, what does Kant imply by asking how such knowledge is possible? In the case of mathematics and mathematical physics (which is science only as far as it is mathematical [*Metaphysical Principles of Natural Science*, Intro.]) the question expresses no doubt whatever about the actuality of mathematical science—nothing is more certain, and requires the reader's assent more as a matter of course, than that it exists and contains binding laws (B x ff., 20). What the question does express is a very peculiar Kantian approach to what is actual, namely that precisely *because* such knowledge exists it must be given a foundation. We must find the *grounds* upon which that which is actually known can be ours, so that it is not just available but also becomes a firm and certain possession (*Prolegomena* 5). Metaphysics, on the other hand, is not an actual science at all (B 21). Up to the time of the *Critique* there has been, depressingly, no metaphysical law proved for whose contradictory an equally convincing proof cannot be constructed. For instance, it can be equally convincingly demonstrated that the world must have a beginning in time and also that it cannot have such a beginning. Kant calls such parallel opposing proofs "antinomies" or "counter-laws" (B 434). He had been occupied with the devastating possibility of constructing them long before he wrote the *Critique.* Therefore the project of finding the grounds of the possibility of metaphysics will imply bringing it into being; Kant will have to find the first unassailable metaphysics.

Secondly, what does Kant imply in using the word "pure" in the first three questions? We must first attend to the very fact that there *is* "pure"—in contrast to contaminated—knowledge. "Pure" is clearly a key concept of the *Critique of "Pure" Reason,* and it does, indeed, as we shall see, mean "uncontaminated by anything alien" (A 11). We must expect the immaculateness of our conceiving to play a central role in the book. There is a further implication. Pure mathematics and pure natural science have indeed long been actual, while metaphysics (by which Kant at this point understands merely the knowledge obtained by the pure intellect [B xiv]) is not yet in existence among men. Hence the former must represent knowledge which is on the one hand uncontaminated by alien sensation, and on the other *not* altogether intellectual: the implication is that there must be a pure *non*-intellectual knowledge. Indeed, the discovery of a second faculty of knowledge, in every way opposed to the intellect, a faculty capable of pure sensing, was Kant's first critical discovery (*On the Form and Principles of the Sensible and Intellectual World,* 1770).

And finally, what does the juxtaposition of the three questions imply concerning their interrelation? Kant, in explaining how he came to the critical enterprise, attributed his awakening from his "dogmatic slumber," that is, his faith in the traditional metaphysics, to David Hume (P, Intro.). What Kant had learned from Hume was precisely that his own two original preoccupations (the success of mathematical physics and the natural human predisposition toward metaphysics) were deeply involved with each other. For Hume had pointed out that a type of connection between ideas, which is central to all metaphysics, namely that of *cause* and *effect*, could be made neither by mere reasoning, nor by observing events in nature. For no one has ever seen a cause act or an effect ensue. If, for instance, one billiard ball hits another, which thereupon begins to move, a sequence of distinct events can be observed, but no element in this sequence clearly bears any mark of being the "cause" of another which appears as its "effect." In Hume's words: "No object ever discovers, by the qualities which appear to the senses, either the causes which produced it, or the effects which will arise from it; . . ." (*An Enquiry Concerning Human Understanding* IV, 1). But if Hume had thus shown that the central notion of metaphysics is unknowable, he had shown as well that the central notions of Newtonian physics are superadded to its observations; all our sense experience can give us is that nature seems to be in the *habit* (*Enquiry* V, 1) of following certain sequences. But that some of the events of such a sequence are the cause of others is not an assertion capable of experimental verification at all, and yet it is central to Newton's physics. Thus Hume's attack on metaphysics is also an attack on the certainty and significance of science. But as Hume's assault was made with a two-edged sword, so Kant conceived a solution which his questions, taken together, imply, namely, that the defense might also secure both metaphysics and experimental science at once. This would be the case *if the former were nothing but the ground of the latter*, if the new "metaphysics" were to be pre-eminently what is "behind physics," its ground (B 873).

Furthermore, Hume's peculiar proceeding of elevating experience by attacking its conclusiveness confirmed Kant in the assumption that there is only one criterion of certainty and that is *purity*. Nothing that comes to us adventitiously, nothing that is given to us by sense experience from the outside can be guaranteed. For yet one more observation might reveal an alternate sequence which will prove our first conclusions to be neither always nor inevitably true, neither *universal* nor *necessary*. If observational science is to be certain, then it must proceed from propositions which are dependent on nothing alien, which are pure of sensation, that is to say, they must be with us *from the very first*. The Latin phrase for "from the very first" is *"a priori"* (B 2–3).

We may now recapitulate the assumptions to which Kant's introductory problems commit us by studying their final enunciation: "How are *a priori* synthetic judgments possible?" (B 19). We see that this formulation assumes that there *are a priori* judgments, that is, propositions which arise purely out of our own faculties of knowledge. It assumes also that among these some are "synthetic." "Synthetic" means "put together." Synthetic judgments are propositions in which, as opposed to those called "analytic," the predicate does not merely make explicit what is already thought in the subject. They are propositions in which truly different things are put together; we might say simply: *new* or *interesting* judgments, precisely of the sort science is expected to contain (B 14). (We shall leave for later the reason why Kant calls propositions judgments.)

And finally the enunciation of the problem, in asking about possibility, commits us to the grounding enterprise. This means that we accept in fundamental questions the necessity of a perfectly *circular* argument (B 765). For as Kant explicitly shows, to ground the actual means first to find those elements which make it possible; and when we have, with the aid of a lucky clue, found such grounding elements, to show that on these and only on these grounds we can get what we already consider ourselves actually to possess. Critical grounds are therefore in some sense like the "hypotheses," the rationalizing constructs, of astronomy (A xvii). Here, however, the peculiar aptness of the Copernican paradigm begins to come out. Just as Copernicus differs from Ptolemy in refusing to regard his theory as merely another hypothesis but thinks of it as revealing the true nature of the heavens, so those grounds are not intended as mere constructs but as *truths* (*On the Revolutions of the Heavenly Spheres*, Dedication to Pope Paul III; B 800).

Thus aware of the constraints under which we enter, let us pass straight to the central court deep within the dwelling. The enterprise carried on here goes under the name of:

b. The *Critique of Pure Reason*

Kant uses the word "critique" in a general way to mean a radical review of knowledge in terms of its grounds, which, it turns out, are the faculties of knowledge. But in its central use the word has precisely that aggressive meaning which it appears to have. For in the largest middle section of the *Critique*, Kant undertakes the negative work which gives the book its name, the *exposure of pure reason*, the attack on reason when it tries to work on its own. Hence the title of Kant's book has two meanings. It refers both to the destruction of the pretensions of a higher faculty, specifically called the reason, and to the establishment as a ground of knowledge of a lower faculty properly called the understanding. (The latter is, however, sometimes comprehended under the general term reason.)

The center of the book is, then, the scene of devastation. Here we see the ruins of all those former metaphysical enterprises about which the new edifice is built. We know from Kant's early notes that this central portion was preeminently called "Critique" and that a suggested title for the whole work was "On the Limits of Sense and Reason" (Letter to Herz, 1772). The critique here practiced is not the search for the ground of knowledge but the annihilating criticism of any previous metaphysics.

Kant is very explicit about the centrally negative and destructive character of the *Critique* (B 23); it is because of this destructive effort that Moses Mendelssohn called him the "universal pulverizer." Kant regards it as a great purification which must precede the new era. It is a profound reinterpretation of the Socratic knowledge of ignorance, for while the latter intends to prepare a way into the apparently unknown, the critical revelation of the impotence of reason is intended to prevent forever any venture into the provably unknowable (B 786). In his *History of Philosophy*, Hegel, in a penetrating fifty-page review, calls Kantian philosophy "enlightenment made methodical"— the central *Critique* is methodical enlightenment.

In order to understand why the critique of metaphysics is cast in the form of an attack on pure *reason* it is necessary for a moment to look at the form of the book itself. All but the first part of it is cast in the form of a textbook of logic, organized in part like the manual for Kant's own lectures on logic. In fact it recapitulates, with some significant shifts, the parts of Aristotle's *Organon* or "Instrument" for the acquisition of knowledge. As such it deals in order with the elements of the forms of thought, namely *concepts*, their combination in *judgments*, and finally with *inferences*, and the art of argument. (The corresponding Aristotelian treatises are the *Categories, On Interpretation*, the *Analytics* and the *Topics* [B 324].) Kant uses the name *Analytic* for the first two of these subject matters (which I bypass for the moment) and combines the subject of the *Analytics* and *Topics*, that is, of syllogisms and the art of argument, into the huge middle section of his book, which he calls "Dialectic," or better, "Transcendental Dialectic."

The word "transcendental" literally means nothing more than "going beyond." In the language of the schools those terms are called transcendent which intend something beyond sense experience, such as the One, the True, the Good (B 113). Kant chooses a form of this word to mark his overcoming of the tradition. Whatever goes beyond experience is *transcendent* and without credit unless it is a *transcendental* answer to the critical question: "What are the grounds of sense experience?" (B 25, 80). The opposite of "transcendental" is "immanent" or "dwelling within" experience. The critical logic is therefore a transcendental logic, a logic not of the world itself but of the conditions of knowing it; as Kant says, a logic of truth (B 87). As for the word "dialectic," Kant completes the degradation which Socratic "conversation" had begun to undergo in Aristotle's *Topics* (VIII, 1). There the dialectic method of argument is that method which addresses itself to the persuasion of the interlocutor by likelihoods rather than to the production of truth. Kant goes further—dialectic is simply the logic of illusion (B 349), so that transcendental dialectic is the critique of the production of illusory arguments in the realm beyond sense experience.

We possess, it turns out, a special faculty for deluding ourselves (B 353 ff.). This faculty is "pure reason," reason by itself, without any alien additions: human reason on its own is a faculty for—illusion. The problems with which the *Critique* begins, you will remember, could not include the formulation "How is metaphysics as a science possible," since no one could exhibit such a science. What I omitted to say then was that Kant had substituted an alternative formulation based on the human fact that metaphysics has always been *attempted*. Kant therefore regards metaphysics as a universal human activity and asks: "How is metaphysics as a natural disposition possible?" I had, then, omitted the very last statement of one of the problems of the introduction, which is precisely:

How is metaphysics as a natural disposition possible? (B 22)

Human beings, this question assumes, do actually have such an inescapable disposition. For, even in the face of never-ending failure, they never cease to attempt to gain purely intellectual knowledge. (I might interject here the observation that it is a consequence of making a science of the grounds and faculties of human knowledge that they all become universal; no human soul can have a nature basically different in constitution from any other—this might be called the scientific republicanism of the Kantian revolution [B 859].)

We are naturally disposed toward metaphysics because of the peculiar operation of our *"reason"* (B 355 ff.). The reason, a dubious English substitute for the German word "Vernunft," which originally means a faculty for "taking in," is traditionally that highest knowing faculty, which sees directly into things. Kant retains its position as the higher of two cognitive faculties, but this ranking is now degraded: higher means farther removed from experience, from the immediate production of truth—secondary (B 362). As a token of this, its traditional Latin name, "intellect," is taken from reason and attached to that primary faculty of thought called the understanding which we shall look at later. Reason does no original work of understanding. It merely uses the concepts and judgments which the *logic* supplied to it and combines them into derivative ones called *syllogisms* or inferences. This dependent faculty is, however, by its very nature not content to collect and combine the matter supplied, but insists on exceeding itself.

The *Transcendental Dialectic* shows how the faculty of reason, which is beyond experience, is irresistibly, by its very nature, compelled to lose itself in a definite number of definite fundamental logical illusions like the antinomies I mentioned before. Reason does this in the following way. It notices that its chains of inferences seem to run *backwards* in three patterns (B 379). In the first of these, the premises run backward in such a way that each prior premise has a more inclusive subject, as in the syllogism "All men are mortal, Socrates is a man, Socrates is mortal." Here the subject of the minor premise, Socrates, is narrower than that of the major, man. Other syllogisms regress from consequences to conditions as in "if-then" syllogisms. And yet a third group goes from a disjunction to a collection of possibilities, as in "either-or" syllogisms. Now reason is inevitably driven by its own "interest" to do what it is not fit to do: to originate concepts and judgments which it posits as the principles or absolutely first premises of each of the three types of chains. Thus it creates the concept and posits the existence of (1) a very first and all-inclusive subject (2) a very first, unconditional or free condition, and (3) a being in which all possibilities are contained. Such illegitimate creations are called *ideas* of reason, after the Platonic ideas (B 370). Different processes of illusion are associated with each of the three ideas; among them are, as I said, those antinomies of metaphysics which had early disturbed Kant.

Now the ideas of reason are nothing but the logical formulations of three human concerns which together exhaust the field of philosophy. (1) For that subject which is never a mere predicate belonging to another subject but which itself rather supports all predicates is the *soul*. For the soul belongs only to itself, while all knowledge belongs to it. (2) And the condition which itself has no cause but moves things spontaneously, while itself unmoved, describes freedom. (3) And that being which is perfect in containing all possibilities is God. Now in questions concerning God, freedom, and the soul Kant recognizes the total content of all previous metaphysics (B 7, 826). But he has just shown that substantial answers to such questions are beyond our competence. All the old constructions of metaphysics therefore lie in ruins within his own edifice.

This, then, is the answer to the problem: How is it possible that we have a natural disposition toward a study which brings us nothing but undemonstrable, contradictory fictions? Our highest faculty is so constituted as naturally to lead to excesses. It is the business of a critique of our reason (a way to self-knowledge which gives us a radically new version of Socratic ignorance, namely *certified* ignorance [A xi, B 22]) to discipline this propensity by displaying it clearly. Kant's promise that our desire to know will shortly be laid to rest hence appears to be fulfilled.

c. The System

Having briefly surveyed the very beginning and the middle of the *Critique*, the time has now come for us to look at the architectural blueprint of the whole critical edifice, as set out in the last part of the *Critique*. This part, still in accordance with the presentation of the work as a logic, is called the *Transcendental Doctrine of Method*. In his own manual of logic, Kant says:

> Just as the Doctrine of Elements in logic has as its content the conditions of the completeness of a knowledge, so on the other hand the General Doctrine of Method, as the other part of logic, must treat of the form of a science in general or

of the way and the manner in which the manifold of knowledge is connected to make a science. (*Logic* 96)

A doctrine of method therefore teaches us how to handle and how to put together the elements or building blocks of a science so as to make them the mutually supporting parts of a systematic edifice. But a transcendental logic is in a special position. In mathematics and natural science, as Kant observes in a work which is the precursor of the *Critique*, the method is the result of investigations in progress and follows upon the science; in pure philosophy alone "the method anticipates every science" (*Sensible and Intelligible World* 23). Hence Kant also calls the whole *Critique* a "treatise on the method" (B xxii). For the transcendental philosophy, defined as the "idea" of the system of principles discovered in the critical enterprise (B 27), is intended to mark out and secure the paths of inquiry in all the sciences, to be a *Prolegomena*, or preface, *To Any Future Metaphysics Which Can Assume the Part of a Science*. And this is precisely what a method is. But the critical investigation must itself also be somehow directed. That is the function of the Transcendental Method: it is a method of method. There is, however, something dubious about this organization, for what trustworthy method can show one the way to the grounds of trust? Note, too, that Kant calls the critical system an "idea," almost suggesting that it is itself one of those deluding constructs of reason we have just enumerated. The art—note, not the science—of systems is called, in keeping with Kant's edifice metaphor, "Architectonic," or the "master-builder's art," which is the name of the next-to-last section of the book. Here it indeed turns out that reason, the faculty which is "by nature architectonic" (B 502), does ultimately *regulate* all methodical, systematic, that is to say, all "scientific" inquiry, although it can *constitute* no object (B 670 ff., 860 ff.).

But before Kant can treat the system of knowledge he must complete it, for an element is missing. It is supplied in a prior section called the "Canon of Pure Reason." Unlike Bacon's *New Organon* of science, which is quoted at the beginning of the *Cri-*

tique, Kant's new organon of pure reason is an instrument not for positive discovery but for the cure and prevention of error. Such a negative organon (B 25) is called a "discipline" (B 737); this is the title he gives to the first section of the Transcendental Method, which demands that reason be shown to have no legitimate theoretical use. But *somewhere,* Kant says, reason must be a source of positive knowledge (B 823). A method for rightly using a faculty, such as the reason, is called a "canon" (B 824). The section so named in the *Critique* discovers that positive, original, "causal" use of the reason, which is the missing element in the system, in the "practical" realm, in *morality* (also B 560 ff.). This section is, therefore, a clearing made in the *Critique of Pure Reason* for the purpose of laying the foundations of the *Critique of Practical Reason.*

The possibilities of pure reason are now completely expounded, and Kant can give the legitimate table of rational human knowledge or "philosophy" (B 869). It is the transcendental counterpart of the "Catalogue" of histories, intended to direct empirical inquiry, which Bacon had appended to his *Organon.* I shall recount it only far enough to reveal something significant about the *Critique* as a whole. All rational knowledge has either *empirical* roots, which means that it is based on the trial and error of sense experience, or it is purely *rational;* only the latter is considered in the *Critique.* It is to be noted that this fundamental division is antecedent to the inquiry itself. The philosophy of pure reason in its preparatory or "propaedeutic" stage is called "critique." The principles there discovered, when presented completely and systematically, may then be called "metaphysics." Metaphysics has two branches, the metaphysics of theoretical reason, which is, as we shall see, the same as the metaphysics of *nature,* and the metaphysics of practical reason, or of *morals.* The metaphysics of nature is in turn divided into two parts, one dealing with the sum of all *objects given* to our faculty of knowledge. This part Kant calls "physiology," the account of nature. The other part deals with those *faculties themselves,* apart from their object. Kant calls it "ontology," the account of being. Here in the Architectonic Kant reveals in the almost ironically unobtrusively traditional terms the full force of his revolution. The question of Aristotle's *Metaphysics* (VII, i) which has been "in the past as well as now ever pursued and ever missed: 'What is being?'" is now to be answered by pointing at the questioner. *The science of being is to be nothing but the science of inquiring man.*

This brings us to the second part of this presentation, which deals with the Critical Man under five headings: the *Subject*, the *Predicate*, the *Object*, *Experience*, and the *Meaning*.

PART II. THE CRITICAL MAN

The order of presentation will have the form of an experiment in reconstructing the *Critique* which is suggested by the *Prolegomena*, Kant's introductory sketch of the *Critique*, written between its two editions. In this short book Kant pretends to present *analytically*, that is by reducing the given problems to the conditions they imply, the same material presented in the *Critique synthetically*, that is by starting with the first and highest principle, and deducing the consequences. (P, Intro; this use of these terms must not be confused with that by which judgments are called synthetic or analytic, as described above [P 5 n.], or that by which the dissection of a faculty is called "an analytic," as presented below.) Now everyone who has read both works is perfectly aware that they are both equally analytic or "regressive," as any work of discovery would be: both begin with problems and go back to the conditions of their solution, My experiment will therefore consist of presenting the elements of the *Critique* in that synthetic or progressive order which Kant himself never actually followed. I will attempt, as it were, to read the *Critique* backwards, to derive the complete critical man from his principles.

The matters I am about to take up are drawn mostly from those earlier sections of the *Critique* which I have bypassed so far and which are generally and rightly the object of most intense study. Immediately after the Introduction we find, as the first part of the *Doctrine of Elements*, a section entitled "Transcendental Aesthetic." "Aesthetic" comes from the Greek word *aisthesis*, sense, and means the exposition of the human capability for sensing (B 35 n.). "Transcendental," you will remember, means "beyond sense experience." The Transcendental Aesthetic therefore treats of our capacity for sensing without sensation. The posthumously published work of Kant shows that the discovery of this strange capacity came to dominate his attention. And well it might, for it holds the key to his peculiar view of human nature. The second part in question, the beginning of the logical *Critique* (which immediately precedes the Dialectic, the "discipline of reason" discussed above), is called the "Transcendental Analytic." It is a "canon of the *understanding*" (B 77) and contains the analysis of the grounds of our capacity for *a priori* thinking. The first book of this is called the "Analytic of Concepts." In it is found that investigation in the *Critique*, designed, as Kant says, "with some depth," which cost him the most labor (A 98). It is the notorious "Transcendental Deduction of the pure *a priori* concepts of the understanding." It is not a deduction in the sense used above, but a *grounding procedure* in which certain critical discoveries are justified by being shown to be the necessary conditions of the possibility of science (B 117). Considered apart from its systematic context, this "deduction" can be said to establish the nature of the transcendental *self* which is the highest, or perhaps better, the deepest point of the *Critique*. I will draw largely upon it for my synthetic beginning.

The name for that which underlies all else is:

a. The Subject

In the beginning there is the "I," and the "I" is by and for itself. It is the highest point of the *Critique* (B 134 n.); all else is founded upon it. In English we help ourselves over the enormity of such a reference to *"the I"* by saying *the self* or *the ego*, but Kant uses no such substitutes. Wherein exactly lies this enormity of the highest critical concept?

The pronoun which we very aptly call "of the first person" (a person being defined by Kant as something conscious of the numerical identity of its I [A 361]) is precisely of such a nature that no one else, no outsider, can say "I" for or of another. The word "I" is the pure expression of inwardness which cannot become our own or another's object (B 321). Thus in attempting to use the noun for which the "pronoun" "I" stands, our name, we are constrained to shift to another "person," the third, just as we must, in speaking of another, say "he" or "she" or "it." How then can Kant make *the* "I" an object of investigation? For Descartes in his incubator, such a study was still simply and frankly *self*-examination (*Discourse on Method* IV, B 422 n.). One of Kant's great innovations is, as we shall see, precisely to show in what respects we can and cannot observe ourselves, in what way the "I" can or cannot become its own object (B 155 ff.). But because the "I" of the *Critique* is always presented as any "I" in general (B 404), a tremendous fact becomes blurred: there is *no* way the Kantian self can come to know of another self (B 405). It is explicitly disbarred by its very firstness, its radical self-sufficiency, from sharing in the inwardness of another, or even from receiving immediate evidence of another's depth, another's soul (B 578). (Kant ventures the *hypothesis* that in the world of appearance inwardness assumes the form of pure externality, that souls when they appear to other souls do so as bodies [B 428], but that is a conjecture.) It is therefore in the terms of the *Critique* perfectly indifferent whether *its* "I" is one or many, whether Kant is examining himself or *the* "I"; each "I" is universal: all the world there is. (This absolute isolation of the self is connected with Kant's understanding of language, to which he gives only slender attention. Souls can communicate with each other only if language conveys beings of thought from one soul to another. But for Kant, as we shall see, there is no such being and no such conveying. We can see at once that this casts an uncanny light on the book itself—for is it not conveying to us precisely Kant's thought?)

How then does the "I," the original "I," become known to itself? Kant points out in the beginning of his *Anthropology* (I, 1) that the original "I" is not the first person known to us in time, for children speak of themselves in the third person as if they were one among many before they discover that all their judgments, no matter what they are about, have one and the same subject and verb. For all judgments follow after the phrase "I think" (B 131–32, A 354–55). This "I" which thinks is always present (A 117 n.), noting its own activity, and preserving its sameness and singleness through all passions (A 108). It is a final and universal subject which underlies all its own predicates (B 407, P 46). This universal and original person can be active only in self-concern. The name which Kant borrows from Leibnitz for "self-activity" (B 130), for self-attention, is "apperception," or self-perception, self-consciousness. This apperception is *transcendental*, for in attending to myself as a thinking thing I am studying the radically original *knowing faculty* (A 114). At the same time, if knowing requires a "taking in" of an object, as the word "perception" literally implies, I cannot "take in" the very source and support of all my knowing except in a very special way (B 429–30). In an anticipation of the mathematical limit notion, Kant finds such a way (B 311). The "I" which underlies all knowing is itself known as the *limit* of all knowledge, as its pure containing form. My root faculty, my pure self, is planted in an unknowable beyond, and I can know of it only *that* it is, but never *what* it is (B 157). Kant somewhere calls the unconditioned the "abyss of reason" (B 691). Since our own original condition is inaccessible to us, we live over just such an abyss.

But if I cannot know what my ultimate nature is, I can yet know something of its mode and its effect. My self shows itself as that absolute and pure original activity, which Kant calls "spontaneity" (B 130, 428). Spontaneity means *wilfulness*, radical self-determination. The activity which has this character is *thought*, which works its will according to none but its own

KANT'S *CRITIQUE OF PURE REASON*   47

laws: At the root to think and to will are the same. It is this
identification which makes the critical man both the theorizer
of the *Critique of Pure Reason* and the doer of deeds of the second *Critique*, the *Critique of Practical Reason*.

It is evident by now that the "I" has an arena, a kind of the-
atre, in which it works its effects. (Why this should be so, why
there is a faculty of thought, is an unanswerable question [A
xvii], exactly equivalent to the question why God created for
himself, and communicates with, a world. We may go further:
the deep beginnings of modernity are nearly all to be found in
bold perversions of Christianity—the genesis of the critical *man*
takes the form of a *logos*, a sentence such as that by which the
God of the gospel of John launches himself into a world; that
creation is the very model I am using in this development.) The
"I" is thus a universal subject in need of completion. We therefore must go on to:

b. The Predicate

The subject and its verb in the words "I think that . . ." demand
a completion of meaning, namely the thought which the "I"
thinks. Whatever the "I" thinks is *its* thought and belongs to it,
but while it is *of* the "I" it is also *for* it. Our original "I" possesses
a secret power, which distinguishes us from the beasts, a power
of doubling itself, of holding its own activity before itself. It is
this power which launches us on our career as knowers. Anything whatsoever which is there for the "I" is called its "representation" (B 376). The word, again borrowed from Leibnitz,
is unfortunate, since it implies that something which is present elsewhere, outside, is imaged by us or in us. But this is not
what Kant means. Re-presentations are simply presentations,
or what is *present* to us; there is no going beyond them, and they
represent nothing else. (Kant's German term, "Vorstellung,"
which means "something set before" is more adequate.) There
is nothing *for us* which is not *our* predicate. The transcendental "I" delimits an island realm which has only internal affairs.

The first of our representations, that is, those closest to the "I" beyond, are its thoughts (B 428–29). These come into the world of representations as the effects of the transcendental "I" when these are regarded as a root faculty of the soul, as its "modes of expression" (*Battle of the Faculties*, II, end). Kant calls these effects collectively the *"understanding"* (B 93 ff.). It is that primary cognitive faculty upon which the secondary faculty of reason depends, and which, as I mentioned before, is for Kant *the* intellectual faculty. The understanding is the "I" as a source of activity *within* its own world. It is a faculty of representing representations, that is, a *reflecting* faculty. It carries forth the original unity of the "I" into the multitude of its representations (B 105). It is the primary faculty because it governs by establishing relations among, by uniting, by grasping, by "taking together," that is, by *conceiving* our many representations. Its primary and fundamental relating act is that which unites representations by reason of their common relation to the thinking "I"; as Kant says, it is an act "which brings the manifold (that is, the variegated field) of given representations under the unity of apperception" (B 135). This unity is expressed in "judgments" characterized by the copula "is" (B 142). When I think that "this body *is* heavy," I have performed an act by which the singular and single empty representation which is expressed in "I think" has become the vehicle or correlate of two other representations which are united within it. This primary relating function is called *"judging"* (B 141–42). There is also a kind of incomplete judgment in which representations are related not upward to the apperception, but downward only. So, for instance, "body" comes under "heavy," and many more representations come under "body." Such incomplete judgments, which assert nothing, are called *concepts*; these are the isolated acts of the understanding (B 94).

There are a definite number of definite downward unifying *functions*, called the pure concepts of the understanding (B 102). The fact that Kant will name them must not deceive us about the nature of our reflecting faculty. It is a mere or naked power of arranging multitude, of operating or functioning; the audible names of its products convey no real meaning (A 241). (As Kant observes in his *Anthropology* [I, 18], it is precisely because words in themselves mean nothing that they are apt for characterizing the results of thinking.) Thinking by itself is a mere functioning, an invisible empty grasping (A 245); *to think is not to know* (B 145–46). Its grasp must be filled. At the lower end of the hierarchy of concepts there must be some material, something to conceive. And as the Transcendental Aesthetic, from which the following is largely drawn, shows, there is something of this sort. We have a faculty which supplies the material for the formulations of thinking.

It is the *sensibility*. Kant opposes the faculties of thinking and sensing as "outermost extremes" (A 124). Thinking is active and spontaneous; the sensibility is passive and receptive. Thinking is an empty function; the sensibility has a pure original content (B 160). Thinking runs through a manifold, unifying it, and is discursive; the sensibility contains one singular presentation which is ready to receive a manifold, a matrix of particularity and variety. Kant calls this passive power, this faculty for reception, *"intuition"* (B 33). The prefix "in" has here nothing to do with any "insight," any "looking into"—for that is precisely what the receptive capacity cannot do—but has the sense of "looking *at*" intently, a sense clearer in Kant's German word "Anschauung." Intuition is a faculty for formative looking, a capacity for taking in the alien and shaping it into sights for the soul.

Here, at its lower limit, the isolation of the "I" gives way to certain intimations from beyond, from "outside." It is an undeniable fact that we are aware of a multitude of alien and adventitious representations, and that there are far more of these than of those that we ourselves produce and control. How can this come about? The sensibility is not an organ of sense but a formative capacity for receiving the given. Representations do not come to us *through* but *in* the intuition. The sights which occur in the intuition are called *"appearances"* (B 34). In the common understanding the appearance of a thing belongs to *it*; it is the appearance *of* the thing and evidence concerning its hidden being. But the appearances in the intuition are formed and shaped by the faculty itself. They belong altogether to us and are through and through appearances *within* us, not from without, *from* another thing. What then does come from the outside?

Just as the sensibility offers material to the forming functions of the understanding (B 87), so the appearances within the intuition are as forms for a material which Kant calls *sensation* (B 60, 207). Sensation is a representation of the "thereness" of something alien. It is that in appearances which gives them reality or "thinghood," which makes them capable of confronting us as alien and independent "somethings" (B 375). As our representation, sensation is entirely and forcefully subjective. But it is just thus that it impresses us with intimations of an otherness which is there, outside. What does it tell us of things outside?

Nothing whatsoever about their nature. For the appearances of these things are not with *them*, but with *us* (*Foundations of the Metaphysics of Morals*, p. 451), so that these outer things have, insofar as they are considered in themselves, no externality, no covering outer skin, no dress, so to speak, in which to present themselves to us. Things in themselves, outside of us and stripped of their appearance, are pure naked inwardness, as inaccessible to us as our own "I" (B 339). Such pure inwardness, like our apperception, is again pure thought. Therefore Kant calls such things "things of thought," in Greek "*noumena*," while he calls the appearances in us "*phenomena*" (B 306 ff.). Of the *noumena* we know only *that* they are, but not *what* they are (B xxvi, 568). And just as Kant conjectured that our two root faculties might be at bottom one (B 29), so he conjectures that the "I" beyond our innermost limit and the things beyond our outermost ken are one and the same, that we are surrounded by one and the same unknown ocean on all sides (A 379–80). Here is Kant's description of our inner island and the fate of him who tries to take leave of himself:

KANT'S *CRITIQUE OF PURE REASON* 51

But this land is an island and locked by nature herself within immutable boundaries. It is the land of truth, (a charming name), surrounded by a wild and stormy ocean, the true seat of illusion, where many a fog bank and much melting ice counterfeits new lands, and by endlessly deceiving with empty hopes the sea-farer roving about in search of discoveries, involves him in adventures which he can never forego and never break off. (B 295–96)

Our inner island, the scene of appearance on the ocean of darkness, is the one and only *land of truth*.

What is that truth? Kant's definition of truth is perfectly traditional in form and absolutely new in content (B 82 ff.). Truth is "adequatio intellectus rei," the approach or fitting of the understanding to the thing. A thing which presents itself for the understanding to fit itself about, to grasp, is said to be "something thrown out before it," an *"objectum"* or object. Truth involving objects, or *objective truth*, is knowledge which matters, material knowledge which is neither empty nor blind (B 75). Empty knowledge is that in which thinking has no object other than itself, the empty catching of thinking at thought; blind knowledge is the mere unreflected sight of the object. Truth is therefore the *secure* acquisition of something *worth* having, Kant's name for the process of such acquisition is "experience" (B 218), a word in Latin and English reminiscent of the devices for extracting such knowledge, namely the experiments of science.

Accordingly error is no longer, as in the *Theaetetus*, the deeply significant complement of truth, but a mere mismating which arises, together with its pseudo-object, *nothing* (B 347 ff.), on the secondary level of reflection, and for which the critical method can provide a radical cure. For both understanding and intuition are in themselves infallible; error arises only when the representations belonging to one faculty are interchanged with those of another (B 150). Kant calls such an "interchange" by its Greek name, "amphiboly" (B 316 ff.). It is particularly the concepts of reflection, the concepts for thinking about thinking, which are prone to such amphibolies. For since our understanding must always grasp *something*, it tends, falsely, to turn its own thoughts into objects. The highest concept of reflection is that of "something" in general, the others are exactly those which have kept recurring in my deductive presentation: unity, reality, cause, possibility, which are names both of categories *and* of prior critical notions (*e.g.*, B 131). It is characteristic of critical thinking that these must all be used on two levels, (1) properly of true objects, and again (2) improperly to describe thinking itself. But with the critical method to guard us against their interchange the perfect truth of our knowledge is guaranteed. For man, to know is to know completely and certainly. There is no place for opinion (B 809), Socrates's human way station between exposed ignorance and hidden knowledge.

We see that if we are to "be about" anything, then at the center of our soul there must stand:

c. The Object

We are confronted with appearance, filled with the feeling of reality. The German word for such a confrontation is "Gegenstand," something which "stands up to" us (B 242). Kant's usage is by no means rigorous, but he very often uses this word for something *given*, which confronts the understanding, just as he often uses "thing" for the hidden source of reality in appearances. This given something which confronts us is there for the understanding. Blind in itself, it is the potential object of truth, that to which the understanding equates its grasp (A 104).

And now the understanding shows itself to be functioning towards a definite end. For in grasping the appearances, in conceiving them, *thinking itself makes objects of them*. The pure conceiving functions of the understanding have no other purpose than to make the "givens" of our sensibility into objects. But since the grasp itself molds the thing, the fit cannot help but be an adequate one—to be objectively valid and to be necessarily

universal are exchangeable notions (P 19). Our material knowledge is "objective." That means that it is both *about something*
and also *true*, because we ourselves supply its material as well
as its form (B 137 ff.). This form is imposed by the subjective origin of the functions of our understanding, which ensures that
they cannot be altered adventitiously. Hence their enumeration
is available to us and can be once and for all completed. This
enumeration is given in the "Analytic" (B 106 ff.), or element-
finding part, of the Transcendental Logic, which is therefore a
logic of truth (B 87). Using an Aristotelian term, Kant names the
pure concepts of the understanding *"categories."* Furthermore
he gives names, taken from traditional metaphysics, to exactly
four groups of three each. But it is of the greatest importance to
remember that these names carry no meanings and are nothing but labeling characters. We can know nothing objective of
our own thinking functions. For to do that would be to grasp
our own conceiving, to treat the categories as if they, by themselves, constituted an object. But this "transcendental" object
would be a mere "something," really a "nothing" of thought
(A 250 ff.), an empty form. Thus thinking would be attempting
to overleap itself, to transcend its own activity. But "critique"
means first and foremost: the willingness to forgo the impossible. And what is impossible is precisely that we should view
our own thoughts, which are mere functions. As Kant puts it, to
see them we would have to have *intellectual intuition* (B 307), a
faculty which he regards as a contradiction in terms.

The expression of legitimate, material knowledge is the
judgment. In it are *put together* concepts in themselves disparate,
on the basis of an object in which they are united and united
from the very first. Hence it is an *a priori* synthetic judgment. And
so we have come to that concluding point in our deduction, that
point which corresponds to and solves the *Critique*'s introductory problem, "How are *a priori* synthetic judgments possible?"
It is by reason of our very constitution, now brought to light by
the critical enterprise, that we inevitably make objective judgments, judgments which are both about something and also

certain, judgments which are *true*. Here is one of Kant's own examples of such a judgment: "The sun warms the stone" (P 20 n.). Abstract from all sensation, from the color of the sun, the weight of the stone, the warmth of the air. What is left is the assertion that one object is related to the other as *cause to effect* (P 29). "Cause and effect" is the name of that, for Hume, most notorious of all metaphysical notions, the second of Kant's three categories of relation. The judgment asserts that this relation is objectively the case, not merely seemingly so. It could only assert a mere seeming if it depended on sensations, which are empirical, that is, a matter of trial and error, and therefore uncertain (B 142). But *all* objects, not only sun and stone, are necessarily related as causes and effects—for that is precisely what we *mean* by an object. So also all objects stand under the remaining categories of relation. For all are permanent substances which have accidents or changing states, as when the stone, though remaining a stone, *grows cold* at night. So also all objects are related in a community of interactions, for sun and stone *attract each other*. In fact each object stands under most of the remaining nine categories. For in Kant's favorite formula: "the conditions of the *possibility of experience* in general are at the same time the conditions of the *possibility of the objects* of experience" (B 197). This sentence means: we can have material knowledge or worthwhile truth only insofar as we have objects to which to fit our thinking, and we have the latter since our thinking itself constitutes them.

I have said that to come under the pure concepts of the understanding is precisely what we mean by "being an object" (B 125). But we must recall that the pure categories have no real meaning and that therefore the pure object has no reality (A 250). Our final task will be to show how the categories can become *embodied*. This will be the same as deducing our ability to learn by experience, to do experimental science or to be capable, as Kant says, of *empirical thinking*. The deductive presentation will be drawn largely from the second book of the Transcendental Analytic, which is called the "analytic of Principles."

Every concept is a complex of characterizing marks or "notes" common to many representations and may therefore be regarded as determining a *rule* for putting these together under itself. If such a rule comes from the highest concepts and is one of those by which objects themselves are constituted it is called a "grounding sentence," that is, a ground or *principle* for formulating laws (B 188). The categories thus furnish a matrix of laws governing the constitution and power of objects. The system so governed is called *"nature"* (B 263), and the categories are the sources of the *laws of nature*, which are therefore the results of the legislative activity of the understanding. Thus the sentence "the sun warms the stone" is very aptly called a *judgment*, for all of nature appears before the court of our understanding to be interrogated and judged by its self-given laws (A 126).

The highest principle of the understanding is that "every object stands under the necessary conditions of the synthetic unity of the manifold of intuition in possible experience" (B 197). This means that we can have experience, namely pronounce objective synthetic judgments upon our sensation-filled appearances, only because the manyness in our intuition has already been unified, because it has been put together in a *synthesis*. The necessary condition for this synthesis which first makes synthetic judgments possible is furnished by a mediating faculty whose very nature it is to be a common ground (A 124).

For in order for a representation to fall under a concept it must be somehow similar to the concept. But the categories differ from the appearances which they are to organize as radically as do their two faculties of understanding and intuition. A "third faculty" is responsible for that interpenetration of these two which produces a synthesis, a "structure of unity." In Kant's words it is "a blind but indispensable function of the soul without which we would have no knowledge at all but of which we are seldom even as much as conscious" (B 103). It is the *"imagination."*

As the common ground of the other two faculties, imagination is the same as understanding in being actively unifying

(B 162 n.), and the same as intuition in having a given multiplicity of material (B 164). (Hegel, intending to deliver a devastating criticism, describes the imagination simply as Kant's intuitive intellect or intellectual intuition [*History of Philosophy* XV, 570]). This double character is evident in the fact that the imagination alone is "productive." That is to say, while itself remaining hidden, it produces something compacted of form and matter, an appearing *object*. Kant calls such objects the *"schemata"* of the imagination (B 177). To understand what a schema of the imagination is, to comprehend that "mediating third," which is on the one hand similar to the intellect, and on the other to intuition, we must briefly review and complete the development of the other two faculties of the soul.

The understanding, the faculty, so to speak, on the inner side of the soul, had two aspects: the transcendental apperception belonging to the single "I" beyond all appearance and the understanding by which that "I" grasps the many representations of sense. Now it must be the case that the sensibility at the other extreme also has two aspects. One of these faces toward the outer limit of the soul and is ready to receive ever new sensations issuing from beyond. It receives these under the form of externality, which is, as we shall see, the triple extension of *space*. The other is turned toward the transcendental "I" and receives it as an appearance under a single intensive dimension. It is the dimension most appropriate to the original unity of the "I," namely *time*. The intuition therefore has a form of outer sense (of which we shall say more soon) and a form of inner sense. The reflective concepts "inner" and "outer" describe both *whence*, in the topography of the soul, the two senses receive sensation and *what form* they give it (B 373). So outer sense both receives what is alien to us (B 32) and gives it that form which we call "being outside," by which we mean that the parts of the object all lie stretched out away from the outside each other. That is to say, they lie *in space*.

But it is the inner sense which is crucial at this juncture. In it material self-knowledge first becomes possible, for here *we appear to ourselves*; here we can become our own objects (B 156 f.). Kant regards this discovery of the doubling of the "I," which enables the thinking "I" to come to itself as an appearance, both as a mystery and as the fundamental fact of psychology (B 334), since it accounts for the very possibility of such a science. In self-attention I affect myself and am revealed to myself in a *sensual apperception* (B 68 ff.). But such attention yields first of all a representation of *passing time* (B 182). My inner appearances, my feelings, imaginings and thoughts, are borne along on a steady flux in one direction, from past through present to future. This is the form of every inner representation, and since all representations are to begin with *my* representations, all appearances have first of all the form of inner sense—they are temporal (A 99). As Augustine says: ". . . time is nothing but a stretching out, but of what thing I know not, and I marvel if it be not of the mind itself" (*Confessions* XI, 26). In particular the thinking "I" casts its timeless transcendental functions into the inner sense. Here they appear as our ordinary temporal thinking, that synoptic scanning, comparing, reflecting, by which we finally abstract from all the differences of objects to obtain their common concept. It is in temporal thinking alone that change can be grasped (B 48), for in successive times alone can contradictory predicates belong to a subject (providing, of course, that they both obey the law of non-contradiction, the highest formal law of thought, which is that no predicate must contradict the subject [B 189]). Time is here not, as it is for Aristotle (*Physics* IV, 14), the soul's *measure* of motion, but the very *condition* of motion.

Now how can the thinking "I" be said to cast itself into its inner sense? Both forms of the intuition, as formative receptacles, contain a kind of pure content. It is a pure single manifold which is nothing but their readiness to be determined or conceived in a certain way, a material which is merely a potential structure or a system of relations, not altogether unlike the contents of the receptacle in the *Timaeus* (50 ff.). Kant terms these contents "pure intuitions," using the name of the faculty for its material as well (B 160 n.). In entering the pure manifold of outer sense, the faculty of conceiving constructs the empty but determinate objects of geometry. So, for instance, we define a triangle and then imagine it, intuiting properties additional to those in the mere concept (B 271). Thus an *a priori* synthetic mathematical science becomes possible. But since in sense experience it is this very same geometrically determinable manifold which is now filled with sensation as well, pure geometry is always empirically applicable (B 206).

But because the inner sense is the sense of senses, the first and crucial interpenetration of the extreme faculties is that in which the pure concepts of the understanding enter the inner sense. This occurs when the categories determine time, or, what is the same thing, when time determines the categories (B 177, 184). Just before it was natural to speak of imagining the construction of a concept in space; similarly it is precisely the imagination which introduces concepts into time, and its schematic products *are nothing but general or guiding constructions of the pure concepts in pure time.* Clearly the imagination is the *central faculty* of the soul, because it is nothing but the soul's capacity for combining its extremes; it is the common ground of intellect and intuition. And since the inner sense is, as it were, at the topographical center of the soul, it does its hidden first work deep within it (B 181). There it shows itself as the ground and bedrock on which the island of our own epiphany to ourselves, which must precede all alien appearances, is founded.

The imagination can introduce the pure conceiving functions into time only because the pure manifold, being nothing but a system of potential relations, is not, as Kant observes in a pre-critical work, so very unsimilar to a concept (*On the Sensible and Intelligible World* 15). In fact, since the imagination is understood as a faculty of representing in the intuition a confronting object without its confronting presence (a "Gegenstand" without "Gegenwart" [B 151]), pure time, as an intuition empty of sensation, is the immediate "ens imaginarium" or imaginary being (B 347). Hence, just as Kant calls the schema the mediating "third" between intellect and intuition (B 177), so he calls time the "third" which, as the bearer of all our representations, is the medium in which they are put together or synthesized (B 194). This synthesis is the work of the imagination, and its products, the schemata, are those general constructions or patterns into which concepts organize time immediately and space derivatively. Kant calls the schemata "phenomena" in a special sense (B 186), because they are a kind of pure appearance, a pure object, or rather object structure. Such a structure, although it is a no-thing of the imagination, "calling for an object" to be realized in it by sensation, is yet distinguished from the transcendental object by being not an empty fabrication of mere thought, but the first step in the "realization" of the categories. It is the mediating thing to which the synthesis of concepts in judgments can be referred, reminding us that an object is the necessary correlate of the truth-seeking subject.

If I have not listed the categories so far it was because their names were meaningless; they were mere concepts of reflection. But by schematizing them, by steeping them in time, the imagination has endowed them with meaning (B 185 ff.). And now the principles of the understanding, which give, as you will remember, rules for using the categories to constitute the objects of experience, can, by being employed upon the schematized or temporalized categories, also become meaningful. We are therefore ready to show adequately how "empirical thinking" arises, for the deductive presentation of its genesis requires only that the transcendental elements already presented be worked out in detail.

The following section is therefore somewhat technical. In order to bring out the coherence and even elegance of the critical technique, I will conflate and reverse the developments presented in the Analytic of Concepts and in the Analytic of Principles. The result should be a synthetic account of the genesis of "empirical thought." This is an awkward phrase by which Kant means that reflective employment of the understanding on appearances which is called:

d. Experience

The genesis of experience has two sides: we may develop the step-wise synthesis of the *object of experience* (A 116 ff.), or we may follow the stages by which experimental science as a *system of judgments* arises (B 197 ff.). Of course, this does not mean that either the synthesis of the object of truth or the formation of the corresponding principles of judgment is a psychological process of the appearing "I" going on in time. On the contrary, this synthesis first makes the analytic work of temporal thinking possible (B 130): Insofar as temporal learning has discernible stages, their sequence is apt to be the reverse of the transcendental order, for what is first for us is not first in the order of nature. The synthesis of the object is thus rather a single timeless product of the imagination which, because of the mediating nature of the imagination, has a triple aspect corresponding to all three faculties: understanding, imagination, sensibility (A 99). The fundamental rules of judgment, that is, the principles of the understanding, themselves reveal these three aspects to us, or we would never recognize them. (This correspondence between the genesis of the object and the rules for judging it is to be expected, since it is in fact the imagination which plays the role of a faculty of judgment in the first *Critique* [*Critique of Judgment* 212].)

Now since the principles of judgment arise when the imagination introduces the categories into time (for the principles are in fact nothing but rules for applying the schemata), their number and nature is determined by the categories. Each single category is "a concept of something put together," which means a concept of something synthesized in a definite way, a concept of an object. But while with reference to the sensibility the categories are object concepts, by themselves they are also concepts of reflection, for thinking about thinking. This is indicated by the fact that they come under four headings, which, now that the categories have assumed a meaning, it first makes sense to name: there are three categories each of modality, relation, quality, and quantity (B 106). These categorial classes are no longer concepts for *constituting* the object, but concepts for *reflecting* on this constitution; they give the *relation* which the object has to the faculties of the soul in so far as the single categories in a particular class have contributed to its constitution. Accordingly there are four principles of true synthetic judgments (B 200). These say at the same time what role each of the four categorial classes plays with respect to the faculties in constituting the whole of possible experience and also how the single categories constitute aspects of objects. Therefore, precisely by reason of being "the source of all truth" (B 296) in the material or real sense, these principles are also the transcendental truths, the metaphysical principles of knowledge. Here then is the new metaphysics, a metaphysics of physics.

The names Kant gives to the judgments which follow from the principles are, as we shall see, carefully chosen to trace out the steps of the genesis of experience. It is therefore right to follow the transcendental synthetic act and its expression as knowledge *simultaneously*, which means, as I said, that we must read the Analytic of *Concepts*, particularly the Transcendental Deduction in version A, together with the Analytic of *Principles*. In fact, this way brings out something fundamental about the critical man and his enterprise: the constitutive work done by his soul and his knowledge are *ultimately undistinguishable*—the *Critique* cannot distinguish between a judgment as an act and as an expression, for in view of the isolation of the self to whom would what be expressed?

Let us, then, follow the genesis of experience, ordering it from the Subject outward to the Object.

The "I" is the original source of unity in representations, since all thinking is *its* thinking and belongs to one self. All thinking is therefore identical in origin. This identity or self-sameness first makes possible those diverse unifying functions by which understanding conjoins the many representations of the "I." For self-consciousness, by acknowledging all representations as its own, gives them that vertical unity of which the categories are different horizontal aspects. The unity of apperception is what necessarily accompanies every synthesis, simply by reason of the self-consciousness of the intellect which enters into it. Since it is contributed by the thinking "I," this aspect of the synthetic product is called the *intellectual synthesis* (B 151, A 103). And since an object is something in whose concept a manifold of given representations is united, this synthesis, in bringing unity into representations, first makes cognition of an object possible. Consonant with the transcendental nature of the "I," this unity is purely formal. It is, therefore, formally distinguishable from the synthesis itself, in which diverse concepts together with a sensible manifold constitute a material object (B 131).

The intellectual synthesis yields the highest synthetic principle. Stated in terms of the apperception, it is: All empirical consciousness, all my appearing representations, must be conjoined *in one self-consciousness* (A 117 n.). In terms of representations this means that there must be one representation which comprises all others. It is the general one called "something." Now we must first of all know in what ways this something can be in self-consciousness, that is, how a thing may be related to the unity of apperception. These ways are known through the last set of categories, those of *modality*, namely: possibility, actual existence, and necessity, and their schemata, which are: *something consonant with time in general, something actually there at a definite time* and *something existing at all times* (B 184). The judgments employing these schemata are called the "postulates of empirical thinking in general" (B 265 ff.). They are these three: whatever corresponds to the formal conditions of experience (namely concepts and intuitions) can exist at some time and is possible; whatever is connected with the material conditions of experience (namely sensation) exists at a definite time and is actual; whatever is related to something actual by the general conditions of experience exists at all times and is necessary. The last refers only to relations of appearances according to the laws of causality, and means that *if* something is actually there, *then* we can always make the hypothesis that there must be something else actually existing which is its effect. These judgments are called "postulates" because they merely demand the genesis of something but do not anticipate its nature. Thus the postulates of modality add nothing to the concept of the object itself but merely relate it to its generating faculty of cognition. For each of my representations is in my self-consciousness in a different mode, depending on its source. The contribution of the postulates is therefore entirely on the subjective side; in particular, they guide us in employing the most fundamental of all the concepts for transcendental reflection, form and material (B 322). They are called postulates of "empirical thinking" because they require that all faculties take part in the full theoretical activity of experiencing. Thus if something belongs only to the understanding, it is merely possible; if it is connected with the material of sense, that is, sensation, it is merely actual; but if it is the result of the conjunction of perceptions through concepts, and therefore attributable to the imagination, it is necessary. Consequently the most complete kind of empirical judgment is the necessary hypothesis.

The second stage is that of the synthesis proper. Here "synthesis" denotes the *product* of the synthetic work of the imagination viewed not as the mere union of the extreme faculties, but independently, on the ground of the imagination itself.

This synthesis is distinguished from the foregoing as an objective result from its subjective unifying act. It is a determination of the whole manifold of inner intuition considered as a *given* pure material. It is an original ordering arising not so much in the pure intuition as along with it (B 161). Kant calls it the *figurative synthesis* (B 151), for it consists in the schemata or time organizations which together constitute the pure but sensible structure of objects, that temporal form which relates appearances in a regulated time order; the imagination, in producing this structure of object relations, works that thoroughgoing "affinity" (A 122) of appearances which gives them their systematic aspect and constitutes the "form of experience." The categories involved are therefore those of *relation*, namely substance and accident, cause and effect, and community or interaction (action and passion). Their schemata are organizations of time into *determinate permanence, succession,* and *simultaneity* (B 183). The principle according to which objects are judged in this aspect is: experience is possible only through the representation of a necessary conjunction *of sense perceptions.* The judgments based on it are called "analogies of experience." An analogy, understood mathematically, is a proportion, that is, a form for finding an unknown; for instance, when a:b = c:x, then x = bc/a. When the proportion is interpreted as a kind of metaphysical algebra, the sameness of the relations involved is not quantitative but qualitative. Hence the unknown term cannot be constructed from the analogy, but the latter can be regarded as giving a rule as well as a justification for seeking the term in experience and a mark for finding it (B 222). Clearly the analogies of experience are really instructions for forcing unknowns to disclose themselves, for *experimenting.* There are three leading principles for making analogies, incorporating the three schemata: in all changes of the appearances substance is permanent and has a fixed quantity; all alterations occur according to the law of connection of cause and effect; all substances, insofar as they are perceived in space as simultaneous, stand in a relation of thoroughgoing interaction. An example of an analogy based on the first principle would be the judgment: "As accident is to substance so is the altered form of burnt matter to the matter itself" (B 228). This analogy then implies that the quantity of matter is conserved in combustions and in general is the source of all conservation laws. The second principle clearly yields, once matter has been properly defined, the first two Newtonian laws of motion, those of inertia and force. The third yields the law of action and reaction. And indeed, once the critical grounding enterprise is completed, Kant works out the deduction of the laws of motion in *The Metaphysical Principles of Natural Science* of 1786; the axioms of Newtonian science (*Principia* I, "Axioms of Motion") are thus mere theorems of the Kantian system!

The principles of modality and relation are only "regulative," which means that they rule the relation of objects to the subject and to each other, while they add nothing to the constitution of the objects themselves. Kant also calls them "dynamic." For they involve those powers and relations which objects must have whenever they exist, but which, since their existence is contingent, have no being apart from actual experience. The remaining principles, on the other hand, are "constitutive" and "mathematical." For they do refer to the objects themselves, and they apply to all possible experience, since they concern both the pure and the affected material, that is, the mathematical constitution of objects (B 199). This brings us to the third and last synthesis.

This third synthesis, in which the objects of experience are, so to speak, filled out, is the *synthesis of apprehension* (A 98 ff.). As the imaginative synthesis includes the unifying act of the transcendental self-consciousness as a separable prelude, so the imagination performs the separable concluding act of "apprehending" or taking direct possession of intuitions. That is, it brings them into empirical consciousness (A 120).

"Apprehending" is the generation of original inner motion, the phenomenal mirror of "the action of the subject." In "running through" and "taking up" the manifold of the sensation-filled intuition, the imagination at once activates it and gathers it into a unity of intuitions, a connected inner experience. The categories for this phase are those of the first set, of *quantity* (unity, plurality, totality).

The categories of quantity have the schema of *number* (B 182), for quantity in time is precisely such ordered succession as is apprehended in counting. The apprehensive synthesis may then be understood as a connected awareness of the pure manifold of time and space, arising in the soul by a kind of original counting. The principle based on this schema is: all appearances are *extensive magnitudes*. Extensive magnitudes are precisely those whose parts lie outside one another so that they can be counted. This principle governs the "axioms of intuition." They are called axioms not only because they are the source of the axioms of mathematics (B 204), but also because they apply directly to intuitions and are therefore immediately *evident*, for the intuition is the place of evidence: what is "intuitive" is patent to inner sight (B 762).

The combining activity is now complete. There is no additional synthesis, but there is one more set of categories, those of *quality* (reality, negation, limitation), which make it possible for the synthetic structure to be filled with sensation. Their schema is that of *degree of reality* (B 182). "Reality" is that which corresponds to sense impressions. It is that in our consciousness which convinces us that we are up against something alien of a definite sort, a "real" object. "Degree" is the quantity of influence which the outside exerts, a quantity not successively accumulated but there all at once as an intensity of awareness. The principle is: in all appearances the real which is an object of sensation has an *intensive magnitude*, that is, a degree (B 207). The corresponding judgments are called "anticipations of perception." They are anticipations because of the remarkable fact that we can know *a priori* one aspect of something which by its very nature we must wait for and receive *a posteriori*, namely sensation. For example, when I come on a body in the dark I can anticipate that its coloration will have some degree of intensity although I can say nothing about is particular color before I see it. "Perception" is *empirical awareness*, that is, consciousness attended by sensation. Sense perception therefore stands at the opposite extreme of pure apperception; but it is to the former alone that the name "perception" (and Kant's German word "Wahrnehmung") properly applies. For it signifies not an activity but a passive "taking in" (attended by awareness), corresponding to the unpredictable givenness of sensation.

This, then, is the threefold synthesis given in the order of transcendental priority: the apprehensive synthesis pre-supposes the imaginative synthesis as a condition, and the latter, in turn, depends on the intellectual synthesis (A 121–22). Each of these transcendental aspects can now appear in time as stages of empirical knowledge, namely knowledge which is "a posteriori," or subsequent to, experience and which uses what is adventitiously given. However, the faculties come into empirical use in an order of immediacy which is the inverse of the transcendental priority: in the learning process of children, for instance, sense perception precedes empirical thinking, and the latter, the power of making objective judgments, precedes full self-consciousness (*Anthropology* I, 1). Hence arise the various versions of the universal pre-critical illusion which takes the child's course for the human way, and regards truth as somehow *given to* rather than *constituted by* the soul.

To recapitulate the empirical syntheses in the order of temporal priority: When possible experiences are, so to speak, activated, the empirical self first becomes conscious of the synthesis of apprehension. This synthesis is a scanning process consisting of a succession of instantaneous views by which the self takes hold of the manifold spatial scene and the sensations it brings with it; this means quickly running over and picking up a series of aspects, for instance, of a house, including its dimensions and colors, to obtain a *synopsis* (A 97) of the accessible whole. The synthesis of the productive imagination appears as *memory* in which past representations, connected by association, are related to the present self, so that it can encompass stretches of time; Kant calls this process imaginative "*re*-production" (A 100). Finally, the intellectual synthesis, the source of cognition, has its empirical counterpart in our ordinary thinking process, in which we scan our representations for what Kant calls a "*re*-cognition" (A 103) of their affinity. But such recognition is precisely the process of forming concepts on the basis of experience (B 134 n.). And so we have finally come to actual empirical thinking, to the well-founded effort to discover specific laws through adventitious sensation (B 165). This effort is the temporal beginning of all our knowledge, though *not*, as we learn on the first page of the *Critique* (A 1), its source.

Empirical thinking is now fully grounded and we have come down to the point where the first problems with which the *Critique* begins, the problems concerning the possibility of science, can arise. And now we must ask: *Why* did Kant undertake this great grounding enterprise in the course of which the critical man arose? Was it really to secure the certainty of science? But that, as I have pointed out, was assumed to begin with by the very posing of the problems. Perhaps it is not the certainty but the *significance* of the new science which is at stake. If that is so, the ultimate question which the *Critique* answers is: "What is nature to us that we should need or wish to know her?" This is the very question whose answer Kant emphasizes in a short addition he made in the second edition to the end of the section from which this synthetic presentation is reconstructed, The Transcendental Analytic. It brings us to:

e. Meaning

Our inner sense is the sense of senses (B 50), but, as the steady unchanging form of our flowing inner appearance, as *time*, it does not itself appear (B 219). Our one-dimensional temporal self, ever slipping away, is by itself incapable of duration; measured time, determinate durations, can appear only against an empirical representation of permanence. Kant remarks how empty a science pure psychology must ever be since in its single dimension that which makes a science scientific, the use of mathematics, is impossible (A 381 ff.; *Metaphysical Principles of Natural Science*, Intro.). For that a substantial appearance is needed. The metaphysical place of "phenomenal substances" is outer sense (B 291 ff.). The form in which we intuit otherness is that of externality, of three-dimensional space. It is crucial to understand that things are not "outside" us because they have a place within space but that they appear spatially because they appear in that sense which is receptive to otherness (A 385). Nowhere does critical self-knowledge demand a more dizzying revolution than in making us aware that we do not look *out into* an outside which is in itself and absolutely there (A 375), but that our seeing is altogether an inner capacity for receiving unshaped sensations in a spatial form (A 370). For we have the satisfying uncritical illusion that appearances come to us *from* things *through* our organs of sense, particularly of sight. But our outer sensibility is no such organ but more like Newton's divine "sensorium" (*Optics*, Quest. 31), in which the whole spatial world is at once *in* and *present to* God, as his self-created representation. The critical man is just such a divinity, a circumstance of which Kant shows himself aware in the work which is the precursor of the *Critique* (*On the Sensible and Intelligible World* 23). Kant's formulaic description, which draws attention to the full force of his revolution, is that space is *empirically real*, since it contains intimations of an outer reality in the form of definite given appearances, but *transcendentally ideal* (B 44), since it is a mere idea and, apart from being a form of knowing, a nothing of thought. Appearances in space have therefore a certain structure merely by reason of the spatial form which received them. They have first of all, of course, their three dimensions (B 41), a structure seen in its pure form in the mathematical objects which the understanding, functioning, for example, with concepts such as "three-sided rectilinear figure" and the solids built from them, may "construct" in the intuition (B 741 ff.). And this solidifying dimensionality of space, though not the source, is yet the condition of possibility of a matter anchored in the three extensions of space and permanent in quantity. Such matter is therefore capable of appearing as a substance underlying all changes in state (B 183). The system of all such permanent things with their alterations and their relations of causality and community is, as we have seen, precisely what Kant calls *"nature"* (P 16, B 263). Its delimitable parts, the things or objects of nature, have the name of *"bodies"* (A 106). Bodies alone furnish us with that permanence against which we can measure our own duration and flux. Bodies, again, teach us all we can know of cause and community (B 293). *In nature alone we know ourselves* (B 276). Nor ought this to be very surprising, since pure nature herself was constituted by the transcendental "I" functioning within itself, and is therefore nothing but the diversifying mirror of its unity. Kant significantly uses the same language in describing both the transcendental "I" on the one hand and body as permanent appearing substance on the other. For he calls both the steady *correlate* of all my appearances (A 123, 183). So also the thin-flowing, appearing "I" *seeks to find itself in extensive solidity* (A 381). This is why Kant calls both the transcendental "I" and the question concerning nature the "highest point" of the *Critique* (P 36).

The true purpose of the *Critique of Pure Reason* is therefore not to guarantee the certainty of science—for this certainty is itself its most certain assumption—but rather to insure that science be an everlasting enterprise in self-knowledge. It is, for Kant, *the* never completed human activity (A 1) in which alone the self can find itself, can procure for itself the stuff through which it feels itself to exist, the mirror in which it assumes a shape. For the enterprise of metaphysics is shortly to be completed, and thereupon the human desire to know what is beyond nature will have been completely satisfied by being shown its hopelessness. There remains the inexhaustible indulgence of our curiosity, insatiable for that experience which alone makes us appear to ourselves (B 255, 334). There is evidence in the work of his old age that Kant finally cared even more about such material self-knowledge than about the formal self-determination of his morality (see my ch. 6, "Kant's Afterlife").

This, then, is the final significance of Kant's "Copernican Revolution": that man literally and exactly finds himself in the bodies and their motions which constitute nature, so that natural science alone provides a sort of self-knowledge. For in studying the world of nature man studies his own creature and image; here he finds what he can appropriate, because it is his own. In the posthumously published notes for the work on the transition from the metaphysics of nature to physics, which Kant, significantly, regarded as his most important and final achievement, there occurs an isolated phrase, revealing and awe-inspiring. It says simply: "I, the proprietor of the world."

3

WHAT IS A BODY
IN KANT'S SYSTEM?

I. THE REASON FOR THIS INQUIRY

I shall begin by explaining why I have chosen to inquire into
the place and meaning of body in Kant's system. There is an
essay by Kant entitled *Concerning the Noble Tone of Late Raised
in Philosophy*. In this essay Kant points to Plato and Pythagoras
as the partly unwitting progenitors of those who philosophize
in a certain elevated and enthusiastic mode. "The philosophy
of Aristotle, on the contrary, is work," he goes on to observe
in sober praise. And he calls Aristotle "an extremely prosaic
philosopher," adding that "at bottom, after all, all philosophy
is prosaic." What characterizes Aristotle's philosophical work
is that it is an acute and serious analytic and synthetic labor

This essay was first published in *The Independent Journal of Philosophy* 3:91–100
(1979).

performed by the pure intellect, resulting in a useable product, such as a preliminary table of categories, which provides the materials for a later worker to employ systematically (B 107).[1]

I have begun by citing this essay because my inquiry will unavoidably issue in the question whether philosophy should be prose and work or perhaps something else. And furthermore I feel obliged to set off the spirit of my present undertaking from that of philosophical "work." For I came on my question concerning body not at all in the orderly progress of formulating and pursuing a philosophical task, but in a most non-systematic way: by attending to certain particular sections and sequences in Kant's work which struck me with a sense of amazement and revelation as well as a conviction that through these passages there might be access to the unfounded foundations of Kant's edifices. As a result it now seems to me that the marvel of Kant's thought lies in the very circumstance that in the name of completeness it throws open dizzying depths for inquiry.

Let me begin by setting out the items entering into this conviction and by showing how they all implicate body in the crux of Kant's effort.

II. THE ENDS OF THE *CRITIQUE OF PURE REASON*

The first of such clues comes out of the very plan and the implied ends of that encompassing systematic edifice, the *Critique of Pure Reason*.

This first of Kant's three critiques has two great ends. The central end is "critical" in the proper, ordinary sense: human reason is *exposed* as a faculty for a definite and inevitable system of illusions. In striking these down, Kant makes a clearing for the possibility of disillusioned human action, performed in the

---

[1] A and B indicate the first and second editions of *Critique of Pure Reason* respectively (1781 and 1786). Other references: FMM, *Foundations of the Metaphysics of Morals* (1785); MFSN, *Metaphysical Foundations of Natural Science* (1786), trans. James Ellington (Library of Liberal Arts, 1970); MFDR, *Metaphysical Foundations of the Doctrine of Right* (1797); OP, *Opus Postumum* (see my ch. 6, "Kant's Afterlife").

face of the defects of human reason. This possibility is worked out in the second critique, the *Critique of Practical Reason*.

The encompassing task, however, is Kant's review of the grounds of human knowledge. Such a review is called a "critique" in a sense more peculiar to Kant, and its determined end is the certification of what we call, simply and grandly, "science," and in particular, of *physics*, as the single truth-producing effort. To say the same thing in other words: the positive critical enterprise is the establishment of "experience." Experience is the joining of the grasp of understanding with some "empirical" matter, meaning something which comes to us, in part, adventitiously, something which is given to us. This product, a grasped given thing, meets precisely Kant's quite traditional notion of truth as *adequatio intellectus rei*, the fitting of thought to thing (B 82). I shall have to return to this definition of truth.

The *Critique of Pure Reason*, then, not only clears the decks for the practical use of our reason, but also provides the foundation for its theoretical use, and this latter part contains the great positive discoveries of the book. In considering this twofold, this positive and negative end of the work, the moving enigma of the present inquiry arose. Let me explain.

The first critical system, that which underlies theory, is said to be perfectly complete. Its metaphysical superstructure is a mere work of fleshing out, to be left largely to pupils. Philosophy is essentially finished (B 884). The second critique, the *Critique of Practical Reason*, most explicitly contains no new truths nor any promise of new truths; it merely formulates the full meaning of what, according to Kant, we all know even before any philosophical intervention: that we must do as we ought rather than as we want if we are to respect ourselves (FMM, Sec. I). Therefore its effect on our lives is not to give them a particular content but only a form: Whatever we do, we must do it as beings whose reason is a ruler. Hence neither of these two critical systems presents in itself a working project for human reason.

In the third critique, the *Critique of Judgment,* Kant gives the transcendental principle which permits us to reflect on the empirical particulars of nature and to judge to what general empirical laws they give rise. Thus this critique deals with the *discovery* of natural laws by the judgment as opposed to their *making* by the understanding.

And yet this work has less to say concerning the enterprise of physics than one might expect. The reason is that its principle, aside from allowing us to judge nature as beautiful, is confined in its application to that small domain of organic "products" which are the objects of biology (and perhaps to crystals). These, the principle says, cannot be understood unless they are viewed *as if* they had been furnished to our cognition by an understanding. That is to say, they display, not indeed a determinate purpose, but a form which seems intended to be intelligible. In Kant's term they are "purposive" (Intro., IV). Beyond this principle, there is no doctrine of discovery, so that this critique has no sequel parallel to the doctrine of body.

The reason for this lack is that the judgment adds nothing objective to nature; its principle is purely subjective—it tells us not what nature is but only how we must begin if we wish to understand a certain part of it (Preface).

This circumstance hints how the third critique fits into my present argument, which is that the study of nature is the study of the self in appearance: That domain of nature which invites interpretation by means of purpose mirrors the *intention* of our understanding to find at least some specific appearances conformable to its laws. (For there is no guarantee that beyond the basic laws of matter, empirical nature will prove amenable to science.) Hence in the organic domain we appear to ourselves insofar as we *desire* to know, for here nature in showing design, that is, in appearing to wish to be understood, mirrors the design our understanding has on knowledge. In respect to nature's "analoga to life" Kant for once grants the theoretical faculty a desire, a will, a life of its own. Hence this aspect of the discovery of nature, and no other, gives pleasure (Intro. VI).

The theoretical enterprise which is founded in the first critique does, on the other hand, provide our lives with an infinite and legitimate business, namely physical science. Now having expended a truly enormous effort on properly founding such work and on showing that reason has no other, does Kant glory in its beauty, praise its pleasures, demand that its modes inform public and private life? In Plato's *Timaeus*, for instance, which, somewhat anachronistically speaking, also contains a theory of science, the enterprise is accepted by Socrates as "a feast of accounts" (27 b) and a celebration. So completely does Kant omit all comment on the human significance of this single vast permissible use of the human understanding that his omission arouses suspicion of an issue too deep in the foundations of the system for a merely passing explanation.

I shall state right away that I believe there to be evidence, not peripheral and subtle, but bold and central, that in Kant's system physics as the science of bodies does indeed play a central human role, *for it is the one access we have to our own souls and provides all the self-knowledge we can have.* I cannot tell why Kant never explicitly drew attention to this circumstance in all its pathos, except by noting that all great philosophical works that I know have these telling lacunae, junctures too sensitive, deep and dangerous to bring out in words.

III. THE GRAND DESIGN FOR THE DEDUCTION OF PHYSICS

Let me now adduce somewhat more external evidence for the overwhelming importance which the science of bodies has in Kant's system by sketching out the intention not of one work, but of a sequence of three works which largely occupied his later years. This sequence contains a grand design for the *deduction of empirical physics*, an apparent contradiction in terms, which the setting out of the design will be only partly able to reconcile.

The first of the texts in question is again the *Critique of Pure Reason* and within it the section called the "Principles of the

Understanding." One form of the principal proposition of the understanding is: "The conditions of the *possibility of experience in general* are at the same time conditions of the *possibility of the objects of experience*" (B 197). That is to say, the foundations of science are simultaneously the conditions of its objects, namely bodies, so that physics and bodies are established together. Both are the ultimate result of the same long deduction. The "Principles of the Understanding" only establish experience and its objects *in general*. By objects "in general" Kant means pure, *a priori*, transcendental (all terms of privative meaning, signifying respectively *free of, before* and *beyond* all sensation— that of which we ourselves are the source). Such general objects are called *things*, and, in their proper complex of lawful relations, they are called *nature*.

The next work in the sequence, which is in the great critical design parallel to the work on the metaphysics of morals, the *Metaphysical Foundations of the Doctrine of Right and Virtue* (5), is called the *Metaphysical Foundations of the Science of Nature*. In this work the outline of the metaphysics of physics is laid down. By a "metaphysics" Kant means the plan of a completed system of pure rational cognition proceeding by specification from the critical preparation. The metaphysics of nature (or of physics—again, the object has the same foundation as its science) is therefore the specification of the "general object" established in the first *Critique* by the introduction of an empirical concept, namely *matter* understood as the "movable in space." And so we have a "metaphysics of corporeal nature" or a "doctrine of body" (MFSN 469), a pure science resulting from the application of the transcendental principles to an empirical concept.

I shall give the contents of the *Metaphysical Foundations* in the briefest outline and return to the work later. In it matter, the movable in space, is treated under four headings: (1) insofar as it is merely movable, (2) insofar as it fills space, (3) insofar as it moves other matter, (4) not as it is an object of experience, but as it is related to a knower, a subject, and his faculties of knowledge.

I should add that the title of this work, of which a reasonable alternative translation is the *Metaphysical Principles of Natural Science*, also indicates a corrective purpose besides the positive systematic one. It is intended to oppose the implications of the title Newton gave to the work in which he presented the very physics Kant is grounding: the *Mathematical Principles of Natural Philosophy*. Kant will contend emphatically that it is not mathematics which furnishes the principles of philosophy, but, in a carefully limited sense, the converse—mathematics is not usable in natural science without a metaphysical foundation (OP 21, *e.g.*, 72).

When we come to the third work in the critical design, there is no longer a parallel text dealing with the metaphysics of morals. This is in a most general way quite understandable, for the theory of practice by its very nature comes to an end in deeds, whereas the theory of experience merely issues in further theory. In any case, in his old age Kant was preoccupied principally with making notes for what he expected to be his most important work, the completion of the deduction of experimental physics. This enormous agglomeration of observations, including also much extraneous material, became known as the *Opus Postumum*. Kant called his projected work the *Transition from the Metaphysical Foundation of Natural Science to Physics*. His great concern was that there should be no jump or discontinuity in the systematic deduction of the empirical investigation of corporeal nature. (I should note here that the word "deduction" is mine, not Kant's, and that I am using it, legitimately I think, in the sense in which one might speak of the deduction of Euclidean from projective geometry, meaning a specification of general principles to yield a more particular system.)

What Kant intended to provide in this "Transition" was an anticipation of all the possible findings of physics, an anticipation which he considered possible by virtue of its systematic character, and necessary to its preservation. Kant's metaphor for a system is that of a work of architecture, in which the foundations, the groundwork, determine a unified superstructure.

The non-metaphorical description is in terms of principles and their ruling power; a system is a universe *pervasively* formed by its fundamental laws, which determine at once the nature of its parts *and* their relations. I should add that for Kant thought is such that to think and to make systems are one and the same operation. A successful "Transition" would have been the confirmation of the systematic character of Kant's groundwork.

Now the anticipation of physical inquiry amounts to an exhaustive classification of all conceivable forces, forces being the ultimate concern of physics, as we shall see. Such a "topic" of forces is intended to direct and regulate all future investigation. I shall not go into this classification very far, because there is a sense of failure over the whole unwieldy enterprise, due both—perhaps—to Kant's failing powers and, again as we shall see, to the inherently limitless and self-defeating character of the attempt to direct experimentation *a priori*.

Aside from corroborating that the impulse and concern of Kant's system really is the science of bodies, the *Opus Postumum* is most intriguing for the telling glimpses it gives of the *motives* of this concern. The "critical" aspects of the *Opus* are dominated by the theme of *self-determination, self-affection,* and *self-knowledge*, by the way in which the "I" becomes the "proprietor and originator" of my world. Kant himself makes an elliptical statement concerning this matter well worth quoting:

> First the consciousness of oneself as a faculty of representation, second the determination of oneself as a function of oneself, namely a force (vis) of representation. Third the appearance of oneself as a phenomenon, as a manifold of representation: a thoroughgoing determination of oneself, but only as appearance and not as a thing in itself; objectively = x, but as the subject is affected by the understanding: *knowledge of oneself through self-determination in space and time.*

The importance of this passage to my exposition becomes clear if I anticipate myself by stating that self-determination in space *and* time is precisely physics—*the science of body is the science of self.*

I shall however base my argument for this statement not on the *Opus Postumum*, but on the vigorous and completed works published by Kant himself.

IV. THE IMPORTANCE OF BODY IN THE *CRITIQUE*

Having sketched out in a very external way the deduction of physics through three works, I must now return to the importance of body within the *Critique of Pure Reason*. To make my argument I must give a very brief review of certain fundamental critical items.

In accordance with the notion of truth set out before, the human soul contains two great faculties. When I say "I think," I mean that I perform a fixed number of definite functions. The system of these operations of thought, which Kant terms "categories," is called the "understanding," which grasps or conceives an object. It is the first faculty. The second faculty is receptive; it provides the form under which what is given to be grasped can be received. It is called the "sensibility" and yields, in Kant's term, "intuitions," that is, sights. This passive faculty is Kant's most crucial critical discovery. It is not strictly speaking a "faculty" at all but a formative receptacle for "sensation," which is Kant's term for whatever is adventitious in human experience. But, again paradoxically, it also contains an *a priori* given, a "pure intuition" or transcendental material, a pure structure of relations, as it were.

The sensibility, in turn, has two aspects or faces, an outer and an inner sense. I shall leave the outer sense, which Kant terms "space," for later and now describe briefly only the inner, which Kant terms "time."

Time is nothing but our capability for receiving our own original transcendental self, that is, our thinking self, as an appearance. It is "the intuition of ourself and our inner condition" (B 49). "Every act of *attention* can provide us an example"

(B 157) of the act of self-affection in which we appear to ourselves. And when we examine the character of our intuition of ourselves as originators of thought we find it to have the form of a flow of "nows"; consciousness is precisely the stream we call time; to appear to myself means to activate or determine my sense of time.

Here I must interject a note on the particular text which I am going to deal with. The part of the *Critique* which is the prime source of what follows is that section called the "Analytic of Principles" of the understanding. Here those two totally disparate faculties, the understanding and the sensibility, are brought together by a third power, hidden and mysterious (B 181), which Kant terms the "imagination."

By means of this faculty the understanding grasps, or casts itself into, the pure formal material available in the sensibility—but only into its inner sense, *only into time*. The products of this injection of thought into time are called "schemata." Thus schemata are thought-informed structures of time, or, equally, temporalized operations of thought. The example of a few schemata will make immediately plausible the claim that they are nothing but the pattern under which our thinking appears to ourselves. For instance, our consciousness is understood by us to be fuller or emptier down to vacuity—here we have the appearance in time of that function of the understanding called the category of reality, which is the thought-function corresponding to a given object; the resultant temporal thought structure is the schema of something insofar as it fills time, the waxing and waning materiality of our consciousness (B 182). So also our consciousness itself subsists: "Time itself does not run out, but in it the existence of what is mutable runs on" (B 183)—here we have the appearance of the category of substance in time, and the resultant schema is that of the permanence of something real in time. In a like way arise those familiar and inevitable patterns of our temporal thinking by which we consider accumulated moments of attention, namely *number*, and contemporaneous interaction, namely *simultaneity*, and rule-governed succession, namely *cause* and *effect*.

With the schemata set out, the principles of the understanding are then simply a set of fundamental rules. These rules demand that, and also tell how, these time-involved categories must now in turn be introduced into *space*, so that an object of "experience," that is, of truth or of science, may arise. They are then, in accordance with the chief principle quoted before, at the same time the rules for the constitution of the objects of experience and for any possible true account of them.

This peculiar sequence, in which the categories are *first* brought together with time and only then with space, indicates that time is the sense of senses, the primary form in which *everything* that presents itself to us at all first appears:

> But since all representations, whether they have outer things as objects or not, belong in themselves, as determinations of the soul, to the inner state, while this inner state belongs . . . to time, it follows that time is an *a priori* condition of all appearance in general, that is, the immediate condition of the inner appearance (of soul) and because of this also the mediate condition of outer appearances. (B 50)

And yet there can be no science of the soul appearing in time as there is a science of the body appearing in space. Nominally, the science of nature, as the study of all appearances, includes both, but Kant makes it very clear that there is not now and never can be a science of soul, a "psychology." The reason is not merely that other thinking subjects will naturally not submit to, or if they do, will not remain unaffected by, our investigations; rather it is inherent both in the poverty of time itself and of the lawless variability of its contents (A 381).

Kant claims (we shall see later why) that science is science only insofar as there is mathematics in it, preferably geometry. Now the geometric image of time is the flowing line of single dimension, which shows how mathematically poor psychology must be when compared to three dimensional space (MFSN 471). It follows that no self-knowledge of interest can come through the study of soul *as it appears*. I must add that Kant forcefully proves that it is an illusion of reason to think that the soul can know itself *as it is in itself* (B 399ff). *Self-knowledge seems to be altogether precluded.*

And now we must look at two sections Kant added to the "Analytic of Principles" in the second edition of the *Critique,* the "Refutation of Idealism" and the "General Note to the System of Principles." In these additions Kant endeavors to supply a place where we may look to see ourselves fully and satisfyingly. This place is the outer sense, *space.*

The outer sense is the second face of our sensibility, a receptive form for all that is other than ourselves, for all that comes from the outside to affect us, for *sensation* proper. But outer sense is also, in inexplicit but apt reflection of this purpose, the source of the most telling feature of all the objects within it, which is that they have their parts outside and beside one another and are *extended* in three dimensions. Thus it is the very structure of the form of outer sense which not only guarantees but even requires that spatial objects shall be subject to geometry—hence Kant's requirement that natural science be geometric is really the same as his claim that it can only arise in space. (It is of course also numerical, since all the contents of outer sense appear in inner sense or time as well, and number, it will be remembered, is a time schema.)

To return to the additions to the text with which Kant decided to conclude the section on the application of the temporalized categories to space. Here he says that it is noteworthy that "in order to understand the possibility of things according to categories, and so to display the *objective reality* of the latter, we need not only intuitions, but even always *outer intuitions*" (B 291). So, for instance, in order to give objective reality to the concept of substance, we need an intuition in space, namely matter, because that alone determines permanence, while time

is in constant flux. Even to grasp our own changing consciousness we need to imagine it is as a line in space, and "the real
reason for this is that all alteration presupposes something permanent in the intuition, but that in inner sense no permanent
intuition at all is to be met with" (B 292). And Kant concludes:

> This whole observation is of great importance . . . in order
> to indicate to us the limitations of the possibility of such
> knowledge whenever there is talk of *self-knowledge* out of
> mere inner consciousness and the determination of our na-
> ture without the aid of our outer empirical intuitions. (B 293)

Outer empirical intuitions are, as we shall see, bodies. Kant
is therefore saying that bodies are the necessary conditions
of our steady presence before ourselves. *They are the sole place
where we appear to ourselves and in them lies our substance.*[2]

V. THE USE OF THE TERM "BODY"

At this point I would like to interject an observation on the
word "body" which I have used in posing my question: What is
a body in Kant's system? Kant himself calls the science founded
in the *Metaphysical Foundations of the Science of Nature* a "doctrine of bodies," so the word seems perfectly appropriate. And
yet it is not a weighty word, or one of consequence, in the Kantian text. Let me give its definition in the *Foundations* (MFSN
525): "Body is a matter between determinate boundaries (and
such matter therefore has a figure)." A quantity of moving mat-

---

[2]It should be noted that this strange outcome is at least consonant with Kant's
peculiar understanding of outer appearance. For when sensation comes to us
from what might be called the absolute outside to fill our sensibility, the resulting appearance in no way belongs to the alien source of that sensation and is
quite incapable of indicating anything concerning the nature of that source
which Kant calls the "thing in itself." It is rather the case that the appearance,
the shaped sensation, is entirely formed by us; one might say that sensation itself
adds nothing but the *fact* of our being affected, the mere activation of the subject (B 207).

ter is called a mass, and so a mass of determinate shape is also called a body (537). Body is therefore a mere delimination of matter; amorphous matter is the basic, pervasive object of interest, whose concept is to be expounded.

Nonetheless I want to hold on to the word "body," for the sake of displaying a consequence of the insistence on founding the science of bodies metaphysically. This is the startling, non-plussing *disappearance* of that inert lump which moves by effort, that shapely solid, that handy repository of trust, that constant object of our most solicitous care, that terminus of an attraction or revulsion (in its solidity wholly different from the *forces* of similar name into which Kant will resolve matter), that whole which is antecedent to any distinction of form and matter, that possible seat of soul which most of us mean when we say "body," and which first excites the inquiry into bodily nature called physics.[3]

VI. THE CONSTITUTION OF BODY

Let me go on now to describe Kantian body as it is developed from the "Analytic of Principles" of the *Critique* through the *Metaphysical Foundations of the Science of Nature*. This genesis is not, of course, temporal, but merely critical.

The functions of the understanding, insofar as they operate on nothing given, enclose in their grasp, that is, *conceive*, an empty object, a mere X. It is only when, next, these concept functions operate on the pure content of the sensibility that a

---

[3]A note to point up the omission of body in its immediate organic sense from Kant's system: I here mean that body which is a living, sensate center of interpretation of other bodies as alive or dead. Kant never, to my knowledge, treats the relation of such a body as *my own* to the transcendental outer sense, to space. In a little work in which the relation of body and soul is indeed discussed, the letter on the *Organ of the Soul*, he says:

> For if I am to make the place of my soul, that is, my absolute self, intuitable anywhere in space, I must perceive myself through that very same sense through which I also perceive the matter which surrounds me, just as happens when I want to determine my place in the body in its relation to other bodies without me.—Now the soul can perceive itself only through inner sense, but the body, be it internally or externally, only through outer senses

material object arises, and such an object of pure material is a pure object of experience, a *thing in general*.

A. "Thing" in the *Critique*

I shall briefly recount the principles by which a "thing" is established. There are four of them, in accordance with the number of basic concept functions of thought termed "categories." Two of these are constitutive and are called "mathematical," because they assure that all things shall be so constituted as to be extensively and intensively measurable. The other two are called "dynamic," because they regulate the relations which all things by their very nature as things must have with each other, and they assure that all things whatsoever shall be enmeshed in one dynamic system, a system of mutual influence.

The first principle is called an *axiom*: It is axiomatic that all things have extension, that all are spatial intuitions and hence measurable.

The second principle is called an *anticipation*: It is to be anticipated that everywhere in space things will have some degree of perception, that is, measurable intensity of sensation.

---

and so can simply determine no place for itself, because for this purpose it would have to make itself an object of its own outer intuition and would have to place itself outside itself, which is self-contradictory.

Let me first comment on this passage insofar as it seems to contradict the "Refutation of Idealism" in the *Critique*. For in that too there is no indication that I am to determine myself as a human being in a certain place *within* outer sense or space, but rather the outer sense *as a whole* contains the stuff which makes my self-appearance possible.

But further, note the problem which Kant evades: My body as an outer appearance has a very special character—it is a kind of sinkhole of sensation; all sensation streams toward it and all existence or non-existence is controlled from it (as when I close my eyes). This is a difficulty for Kant's outer intuition, since it, like Newton's divine "sensory" of infinite space (*Optics*, Qu. 28), ought to be homogeneous, isotropic (the same in all directions), and continuous, while my body and its instrument-like sensory organs represent a point of discontinuity, of preference, and a warping of space. Hence it *does* appear to behave like a *seat* of soul, and this consideration cannot be accommodated in Kant's system.

Third comes a group of three principles called *analogies*: We may infer by analogy that even things not immediately available to observation are bound to each other by definite relations, which are spatial applications of the time schemata, as follows: (1) Time itself as duration is to appear in space as *substance*, so that all things whatsoever will have a steady substrate, a permanent existence. (2) Time as connected succession is to appear in space as cause and effect, so that all things are to be similarly related as causes and effects. (3) Time as simultaneity is to appear in space as the mutual relation of interaction, so that all things are in a like way to affect each other contemporaneously.

The fourth principle is called a *postulate* and adds nothing to the nature of things objectively but only determines their subjective relation to the faculty of knowledge.

Let me review in a little more detail the nature of a thing as it emerges from the so-called "Anticipations" and the first "Analogy," for these are the principles most directly relevant to the bodily nature of things. They provide, in effect, the foundation of "reality" and "substance" in Kant's system of nature.

In the first analogy, in one of those amazing junctures which make Kant's system so suggestive, substance is established as *the spatial representation of consciousness*:

> ... There must be in the objects of perception, that is, appearances, that substrate which represents time in general, and in which all alteration or simultaneity can be perceived by means of the relation of appearances to the same. Now the substrate of all that is real ... is *substance*. ... It follows that the permanent, in relation to which all time relations of appearance can alone be determined, is substance in appearance, that is, the real in appearance, which, as substrate of all alteration, always remains the same. (B 225)

When we recall that time as the pure content of the inner sense is myself in appearance, the statement that *substance is spatialized self* is corroborated. And thus a truly novel meaning has

been attached to an old term signifying self-subsisting being.—
Substance is now the three-dimensional *appearance* of soul
to itself.

In the "Anticipations" the alterations to be predicated of substance are founded, or rather a guarantee is given *that* changes
in consciousness will occur, even though its qualities cannot be
established *a priori.* That we may anticipate that substance will
always be in varying degree sense-activated, that things will
always be sensation-filled, that neither time nor space will ever
be completely empty—this is the critical requirement of *reality;*
reality is the determination of a substance as having *existence,*
that is, as being a thing there and then (B 225). Kant's system
requires that the things of nature be made quick with sensation, that they *materialize.*

B. "Body" in the *Metaphysical Foundations* of the *Science of Nature*

In the *Metaphysical Foundations* the transcendental structure is
realized by the introduction of an "empirical concept," the concept of *matter.* By an "empirical concept" Kant actually means
a "concept of something empirical," that is, a concept which is
in no way the result of observation (though to claim existence
for it would require experience), but rather simply a closer conceptual determination or specification of the transcendental
"thing" established in the *Critique.* The metaphysics of such a
concept is nothing but its full explication. Kant presents the
concept of matter as if he had chosen one of a number of possible instances or specifications of a natural thing (470). But in
fact, it seems to me, no other choice was possible, since matter
turns out to be the unique and necessary first empirical concept
of the science of nature.

Matter is the name—ironically chosen if anyone expects
to be presented with some solid stuff—of the concept of the
"moveable in space." It is possible to reconstruct the missing
reason why the movable in space is the basic concept of the sci-

ence of nature from this sentence: "The fundamental determination of a something that is to be an object of the external senses must be motion, *for thereby only can these senses be affected*" (476, my italics). The moveable is simply that which can excite sensation, sensation being appropriately understood by Kant as that whose very nature it is to be moving and manifold. It remains to supply another omission by conjecturing what specification of the transcendental Kant is actually performing: The moveable appears to be nothing but the real substance of the *Critique*, but now specifically *considered in time and space, not separately but at once*. At least it is difficult to discover any other, truly new determination in the concept of matter.

The Metaphysical Foundations comes in four parts which are completely parallel to the "Analytic of Principles" and are presented in the form of propositions and proofs following from those principles.

The first part, which derives from the principle of extensive quantity (the "Axioms of Intuition"), establishes the geometric treatment of point motions. It deals with the composition of motions in terms of moving coordinate systems, or "spaces," and, in refuting Newton's notion of absolute space, provides a metaphysical foundation for so-called Newtonian relativity. (This is the principle that when bodies interact or are all subject to the same accelerative forces, they constitute a space for which absolute motion or rest are not internally discriminable. *Principia*, Axioms, Cors. V, VI.)

The second part derives from the principle of intensive quantity (the "Anticipations of Perception"), which requires some degree of sensation in things and hence their reality. This part is headed "Dynamics" because it shows that the essential qualities of matter are forces, and *dynamics* is the Greek word misappropriated by physicists for force relations. This part is the most important to my purpose precisely because it deals with the most intimate nature of body.

The third part, which derives from the principles governing the relations of things (the "Analogies of Experience"), is called

"Mechanics" since in it are deduced the laws governing the interactions of bodies in the systems, those "laws of nature" by which bodies are held in systems. In this part Newton's "Axioms or Laws of Motion" are, with certain suggestive variations, completely *deduced* as propositions. Here also Kant draws the physical consequence which follows from his understanding of substance as the steady spatial substrate of all alterations—it is the law of the conservation of matter.[4]

Finally, the fourth part, which derives from the principles concerning the relation of things to the faculty of knowl-

---

[4] A note correlating the Propositions of Mechanics of the *Metaphysical Foundations* with the Axioms of Motion of the *Principia Mathematica*: Proposition 2: "First Law of Mechanics," the law of the conservation of matter; proved, as just noted, by an application to matter of the first Analogy concerning the permanent in space, or substance. It has no explicit counterpart in the *Principia* but is an implicit consequence of the corpuscular view of matter set out in the "Rules of Philosophizing" which introduce the third book of the *Principia* and contain the application of the previous mathematical results to the world of matter. For the hard impenetrable atoms there posited can neither come into nor go out of being.

Proposition 3: "Second Law of Mechanics," a form of the law of inertia, namely that every change of matter demands an external cause; proved by an application of the second Analogy concerning cause and effect. Its counterpart is Newton's Axiom of Motion I, that every body continues in its state of rest or uniform motion unless forces are applied.

Proposition 4: "Third Mechanical Law," laying down that in all communication of motion action and reaction are always equal to one another; proved by an application of the third Analogy concerning interaction. Corresponds to Newton's Axiom of Motion III, the law of equal and opposite action and reaction of bodies.

Proposition 1 establishes as the operable quantity of Kantian physics the quantity of matter as measured by its "quantity of motion," that is matter compounded with *velocity* (momentum = mv). This proposition is formally parallel to Newton's Axiom of Motion II, in which the basic operable quantity is defined as force, compounded of mass and *acceleration* (F = ma). Force as seen in acceleration or change of velocity is simply absent from Kant's foundation of physics, and this omission constitutes the most significant technical difference between Kantian and Newtonian physics.

The reason for Kant's substitution of mv for ma is, however, not merely a technical matter. Kant's proposition 3 begins with the words: "Every change of matter has an external cause" (543). But, as I have noted, this cause is "motion" or "momentum," rather than the force of Newton's Law II. The reason for this substitution is as follows. The two forces Kant has posited in the section on dynamics *constitute matter*, but do not *cause changes of mass*, which is to say that they do

edge (the "Postulates of Empirical Thinking"), prescribes what propositions of physics are to be asserted as possible or as necessary.

To return to the "Metaphysical Foundations of Dynamics," which deals with matter insofar as it *fills space*. It is in filling space that matter asserts its "reality," its power to affect the senses. The universal principle of dynamics is: "All that is real in the objects of our external senses . . . must be regarded as a moving force" (523). "The concept of matter is reduced to nothing but moving forces; this could not be expected to be otherwise, because in space no activity and no change can be thought of but mere motion" (524). Force is the condition of possibility of matter whose possibility is not itself, in turn, explicable and whose concept is not itself derivable from another. As Kant puts it, force itself cannot be made conceivable (513). Recall from note 4 that force for Kant is momentum.

Kant proves that matter is in fact nothing but force by showing that all the appearances of spatial objects are accounted for by forces and only by forces. In the course of these proofs he abolishes solidity, understood as the ability of matter to occupy space by reason of mere existence (498)—an ineradicable aspect, I think, of the ordinary view of body. And he attacks a view he regards as the consequence of positing solidity, Descartes' corpuscular or atomic theory, which asserts the mystery of mathematical and mechanical impenetrability, and requires mere blocks of extension to move each other externally (502, 533).

Matter requires two original forces: a repulsive or driving force and an attractive or drawing force, corresponding to the

---

not affect the motion of "matter in motion." Now for Kant the causes of motions can only be other motions, since a cause is nothing but an appearance which determines another appearance later in time (B 234) and must therefore be of the same kind as its effect. But since the effect is a change in space of a mass, the cause must equally be such an "external" change, namely motion. Consequently in the context of the section on mechanics the dynamic forces function only as mediating mechanisms for the communication of motions. These latter momenta alone are Kant's "motive forces."

two possible directions of interaction between point centers of force (497).[5]

The primary repulsive force is the force more intimately associated with our sensing of extended things. "Matter fills space not by its mere existence, but by a special moving force" (497), which, in resisting penetration, is the cause of palpability. It is, hence, a "superficial" force, a source of surfaces and contacts, which nonetheless constitutes matter throughout so that it is infinitely divisible—there is always a new surface.

On one force alone, however, matter could not fill space but would, by repelling itself to infinity, become dissipated and vanish. Therefore, in order that body might become concrete, as it were, a countervailing original force is wanted. This second force cannot be immediately sensed or even located in a body, but can only be noticed in its effects. It is a penetrating force which does not need the agency of other matter but acts at a distance even to infinity and precisely where it is not (512). Whereas repulsion provides matter with its outside, so to speak, attraction gives it its inner coherence and keeps the segments of matter close or dense. It is therefore the force which, as it binds a body to itself, also holds body to body in a system, such as the planetary system.[6]

Let Kant himself conclude:

If we review all our discussions of the metaphysical treatment of matter, we shall observe that in this treatment the following things have been taken into consideration: first, the *real* in space (otherwise called solid) in its filling of space

---

[5] A philosophical critique of Kant's dynamics is given by Hegel (*Science of Logic*, Bk. I, Sec. I, ch. 3, para. 6, c, Note).

[6] These two forces equally and simultaneously constitute matter—a body is not, as in Boscovitch's *Theory of Natural Philosophy* (1764), a region in space where attractive and repulsive forces alternate, with the repulsive force prevailing and going off to infinity near the center of the body while the attractive force similarly prevails but goes off to zero away from that center. Instead two field-like expanses of force are superimposed and together give rise to regions of various density variously delimited, which correspond to bodies.

through repulsive force; second, that which with regard to the first as the proper object of our external perception is *negative*, namely attractive force, by which, as far as may be, all space would be penetrated, that is, the solid would be wholly abolished; third the *limitation* of the first force by the second and the consequent perceptible determination of the degree of filling of space. (523)

This last "perceptible determination" is matter, while *body is but matter shaped between boundaries* and therefore nothing but a figure inscribed into the continuous expanse of matter: "A body . . . is matter between determinate boundaries" (525). Self-determining solid bodies are simply incompatible with Kant's physical system.

That matter does fill all of space and fills it continuously, so that there is no empty space, is a possibility of such consequence to physics that Kant concludes the *Metaphysical Foundations* with its consideration. Within this work the dynamic plenum remains merely a powerful possibility, and the ether as a special pervasive "external" matter which realizes it remains a physical assumption (523, 534, 563 ff.). But it seems to me that the fullness of space is completely deducible metaphysically from the very constitution of appearance. For it follows both from the continuities of nature required by the principles of understanding (B 281) and from the fact that space, as the receptive form of sensation, can never in itself appear—which is to say that there can be nothing in appearance corresponding to empty space (*e.g.*, B 261).[7]

Its sequel, the "Transition . . . to Physics," shows that Kant himself was concerned about the loss of independent body in

---

[7] I note here only in passing that if a plenum does require an ether, it may well, as an ultimate reference system, be incompatible with the previously established principle of relativity. But this very inconsistency is proof that Kant's metaphysics of nature does not merely ground Newton's physical results retrospectively—on the contrary, it looks forward not only to a physics of force fields, but also to the great ether debate which ended only with the momentous negative experiments performed just a century after the publication of the *Metaphysical Foundations*.

the spread of delimitable stuff. In the very pages in which he now undertakes to show that an ether of some sort is indeed not merely a reasonable assumption but a deductive necessity of the system, he also tries to establish its very contrary, namely natural, organic body. The effort here is to introduce a body which is not merely, by a regulative fiction of reason, subjectively interpreted as organized to serve an end, but which has an objective principle of self-determination, an "inner force" or proper principle of motion, and may therefore be termed "a self-limiting quantum of matter having a certain figure." Kant regards this task as properly belonging to the "Transition." But he also concedes that such bodies might well be "inconceivable," that is, not derivable in the system; therefore, it seems to me, this effort must fail: the system of well-founded matter called nature cannot, as Kant himself has shown in the letter on the organ of the soul, yield bodies fitted by reason of their self-contained unity to be the seat of life or soul.[8]—Indeed, how could Kantian nature contain such places, being itself the epiphany of soul?

VII. THE EXCESSES OF THE SYSTEM

Kant considers that the metaphysical foundations of matter and its science have been laid, and the possibility of knowledge understood as experience is forever guaranteed. Henceforth empirical physics may be safely and infinitely pursued—safely because its principles lie *a priori* in myself so that all experience is self-experience, and infinitely because all of its occasions are excitations which flow to me, with ever fresh adventitiousness, from an alien source.

But at this juncture a difficulty arises. In order for the systematic character of physics promised by its principles to be preserved throughout the enterprise, a regulative framework

---

[8] Another way to put this: Just as physics was rich and psychology poor in determinations in the first *Critique* (A 381), so physics is richer than biology in the *Metaphysical Foundations*.

of investigation must be laid down. The great preoccupation of Kant's later years was to assure the "rational coherence" (MFSN 534) of the science of nature by an ever-closer explication and specification of its basic concepts. The representation of the soul as nature seems to require that *all* assumptions and hypotheses either be soon converted into deductions or discarded. Less and less is left to observation.

To give a prime example: the law of the force of attraction, namely that it varies inversely as the square of the distance between the centers of two bodies, is a specification, *by observation*, of innumerable mathematical possibilities antecedently set out in Newton's *Principia* (III, i–viii, particularly i and ii). Kant too states that "no law whatever of attractive or of repulsive force may be risked on *a priori* conjectures" (534). And yet Kant *deduces* the inverse square law from the mode of diffusion essential to his attractive force together with a fact of Euclidian geometry, namely that the surfaces of concentric spheres increase as the squares of their radii (519).

This ever-growing regulation of observation, insofar as it is attributable to the richness of the system in deductive consequences, might conceivably be simply a sign of its power. And so it would be, were it the case that nature, when arraigned before Kantian reason, the "appointed judge who compels the witnesses to answer questions which he has himself formulated" (B xiii), always willingly and plausibly responded in the required terms. But the fact of the matter, worth far more consideration than has gone into this passing remark, is that physicists have largely bypassed Kant's "topic" of forces and have superseded his metaphysics—for example, its constitutionally Euclidian space as well as the categories of causality and simultaneity—because they considered themselves compelled thereto by nature herself.

And yet it is this very excess of doctrinal consequence which makes the study of Kant's metaphysics of physics the *indispensable philosophical complement* to the study of classical mechanics. For in attempting to account completely for all that is found therein, Kant, even as he fails, unfailingly aids reflection on the terms of physics.

In any case, the failure to preserve the adventitiousness of nature and hence to become a viable guide for experimental physics is only a derivative difficulty of the system. More radical and revealing questions arise about it, beginning with the excessive importance attached to physics as the sole self-study and ending only in questions concerning the nature of philosophy itself.

Let me conclude with the briefest formulation of such questions by returning to the work with which I began, to Kant's essay inveighing against the "noble tone" in philosophy of which Plato is the unwitting progenitor. To one dialogue particularly Kant unmistakably alludes, the *Timaeus* (*e.g.*, in mentioning *ectypia*, and the term "schematized," 50 c), as the embodiment of all that he must disavow in Plato's view of mathematics, of the world of appearances, of truth-telling itself. It is almost as if the treatise on the *Metaphysical Foundations of the Science of Nature* were a specific response to the dialogue—not, however, in the mode of simple diametric contradiction which Kant reserves for his closer opponents like Descartes, but by way of that most radical contrariety which characterizes true alternatives. A parallel study of these two texts would raise the aforesaid questions in some such terms:

Kant destroys *bodies* to preserve the *reality* of appearances, and gives up the self-determining coherence of individual *natures* for an assured perceptibility of *nature* understood as a system of "things." But may not the articulated and distinct beauty of natural bodies and configurations require the intellect to forego sensation-filled dynamic reality as well as ultimate impenetrability in favor of Timaeus' *mathematical solidity* (53 c ff.)? Does not the inexhaustible originality of this mathematicised nature compel us to reconsider whether our sensibility can possibly be the sole source of her forms?

Kant denies the soul a seat *in nature* in order to preserve *nature herself* as the appearance of the soul and the representation of its rational operations. Thus nature becomes a system, an edifice founded on principles and constituted as well as governed throughout by laws derivative from the functions of thought. But may not the curious complex of regularity and irrationality which is the visible world suggest yet a third relation of soul to body, expressed by Timaeus as the *girdling* of body by soul (36 e)? Thus body would arise not as *our own* outer appearance, but as the inner effects of *a world* which is indeed intelligible, but not wholly so.

Kant regards the continuing study of *palpable nature*, the science of body, as the most serious human theoretical activity, and its secure foundation in our own faculties as a completed philosophical labor. But may it not be that the account of the *visible world* is, as in Timaeus' phrase, only a "likely story" (*eikon mythos*, 29 d), and that physics thrives on just those hypotheses, analogies, and likelihoods which Kant disavows in his essay? Then may not this perpetually tentative and open physics be a sort of high amusement with useful effects rather than humanity's central study, and a model-making project—the "story of likenesses," to which Timaeus' phrase alludes—rather than a well-grounded system? Hence a metaphysics of physics may finally have to yield to an inquiry into the nature and being of *models*, which may require the playful poetry of *mere* philosophy as exemplified in Plato's noble dialogue, rather than the working prose of Kant's *systematic* philosophy.

4

KANT'S IMPERATIVE

I HAVE CALLED THIS LECTURE "Kant's Imperative" so that I might begin by pointing up an ever-intriguing circumstance. Kant claims that the Categorical Imperative, which is *the* Moral Law, is implicitly known to every fully-formed human being. And yet its formulation is absolutely original with him. Thus to study that hard philosophical gem, the *Foundations of the Metaphysics of Morals*, the little work in which Kant first sets out his imperative in its various versions, is to be in the curious position of laboring to acquire an utterly new principle which yet makes the *almost* persuasive claim of having been always in our possession. Out of this arises a common experience which, I am sure, you will have—or are already having—with the Categorical Imperative: you will probably find yourself ultimately unable to accept it, but you will never be able to forget it. But

The author delivered this lecture at the University of Chicago in March 1979, at the invitation of Leon Kass, as part of a series sponsored by the Dean of the College and the staff of "Human Being and Citizen."

what we can neither accept nor ignore, it only remains for us to understand. The purpose of this lecture is to offer you some help with Kant's Imperative.

Let me waste a few of our numbered minutes by setting out what kind of help I can try to give you. You might at first smile to hear it, but I think if it is put to you rightly, you might eventually agree that Kant is an easy author, easier, say, than Plato or Nietzsche. He is easy precisely because he seems difficult: laboriously explicit, forcibly systematic, rigorously technical. This is the kind of ruggedness meant to make a text accessible to straightforward explicatory industry. I shall engage in just so much of such explication of terms and their connections (gratifying though it be) as is necessary for our common discourse.

There is, however, another kind of help I can offer, though it might be a little premature. Some people might say that we should go farther in unraveling the text before coming to this part of textual interpretation. It also has to do with the precise sobriety, the systematic self-sufficiency and the deliberate authority of our writer. For these qualities all work to veil from view the real roots of the system—the stupendous assumptions that are packed into its technical terms, the strange abysses opening up beyond its well-delineated foundations, and the human pathos implied in its projects. To raise these roots is not, in my opinion, the worst way to begin to understand the system, and is probably the most profitable way to use our short time together.

Let me end these introductory remarks by pointing out that it is precisely because they have such a rewarding surface and such unsettling depths that Kant's works have attracted the most effective explications and the most pertinent criticisms, among both of which I shall mention only the one full-scale commentary on the *Foundations*, which is by Robert Wolff and is called *The Autonomy of Reason*.

I shall make a straightforward beginning, then, by giving a brief explication of the *literal* meaning of the terms "categorical" and "imperative."

The word "categorical" comes from a Greek verb which means to say something of something or somebody, and to say it flat out, without modification, without ifs and buts, as in accusation. A categorical assertion is an *unconditional* assertion.

The word "imperative" means a formulated command. A command, marked by an exclamation point, is the irruption into the world of an intention, an intention to change the course of events by an imposition of purpose, to cause a re-routing of the flow of events. Not every command, however, has a formula, since it may take the form of an imperious gesture, or an only incidentally intelligible sound, like "Heel" to a dog, or "Let there be light" to the elemental darkness. Obedience to such commands is a measure of the bidder's power to be an efficient cause, to have an irresistibly powerful purpose. An *imperative*, on the other hand, not only articulates a projected move, it also gives a *reason* for it. It conveys not only the what, but also the why, of a command. It is an order directed to a *rational* being.

To understand what a Kantian imperative is, then, we must know what a rational being, a being having reason, is. *Reason* is the chief of those terms which carries in it far more than Kant's bone-dry and matter-of-course presentation exposes. Indeed, it carries within it the whole system.

Reason, then, in its rock-bottom aspect, is first of all a *faculty*, a power. A rational being is above all a being capable of functioning to some effect. Next, reason is a faculty for laying down the *law*, for law-giving. Reason is a legislative power.

What, next, is a law? A law is an instrumental formula that subjugates, or brings under itself, those elements that are reached by it. Yet it does not accomplish this in the wanton, arbitrary manner of a despot, but in the mode of *universality*. The law commands, for it binds (indeed, that is what the word means), but it binds universally, or better, by means of universality, so that in binding it unifies. To say that reason is legislative is to say that it is *the* unifying power of universality. That, in turn, means that it is a power of *principles*, for "principle" is the name in logic of a first law, a law of thought which in unifying all that we have in mind applies universally to whatever may come before us. Let me interject here an observation: Nothing in Kant's system seems to me more difficult to penetrate than his legal metaphor for reason as judgment given under law. I shall bypass that problem here, because its resolution is not immediately required.

An imperative, then, is a command given to a being that is *itself* a source of lawlike commands.

Such a command, to be acceptable, must therefore take the form of a law, a universal rule of reason, or more simply, of *a reason* why that command should obligate any and every rational being. It follows immediately that, strictly speaking, no command can be *externally* issued to such a being; at most a law may be suggested to it for its own internal adoption. What is more, if a law is truly rational, namely unexceptionably universal, it *will* be adopted by any perfectly rational being, and will thus scarcely need to take the form of a command. It will be a principle of reason simply.

In sum, therefore, *a* categorical imperative is an unconditional law-like command, formulated so as to be fit for adoption by a being which by its very nature deals in universals.

The next question must then be: Is there such a command? To be sure, it may seem a little back-to-front to define a formula and then to ask whether it has a matter. The question has a point only because we are all already aware of the fact that *the* Categorical Imperative is Kant's term, taken from logic, for the Moral Law. Therefore the question really is: Is there a moral law and does it and it alone have the form of a categorical imperative? Or, in brief: What is morality?

You may have found the title of the first section of the *Foundations*, "Transition from Common Rational Knowledge of Morals to the Philosophical," a little strange, because it expresses the intriguing circumstance to which I have already referred, the fact that Kantian moral philosophy claims to be nothing but an elaboration of common knowledge. Note that this beginning means that the principal problem of most moral inquiries—are there

moral rules and whence are they known?—is settled before philosophy ever begins: Kant claims that we all know that there *is*
morality; we are all directly acquainted with *the fact of morality*.

This moral fact consists merely in the experience we have
(all of us, Kant means, even the most hardened sinner) of having said to ourselves: "I ought . . ."; *I ought* to do this or that,
quite apart from profit or pleasure, quite against my desires
and inclinations. I must say that Kant's claim seems to me to
ring true: We *have* all heard that contrary inner voice of command, and the moral monster in whom it is dumb is simply not
imaginable to most of us.

Now notice that Kant does not begin with the highest good,
nor with virtue, nor with habits, customs, good deeds or tables
of commandments. (To be sure, we have already anticipated the
fact that Kant will maintain the tradition linking right behavior to commands which is established in the Bible, but their
number, source, claim to authority will all be radically altered.)
Kant, one might say in sum, takes the path of *morality* rather
than *ethics*, where I mean by ethics the concern with *right conduct* and by morality the concern with *good intention*.

Morality, then, or better, moral worth, is the next term to attend to. Moral worth is what is to be valued in the agent's mode
of action. "Nothing in the world—indeed nothing even beyond
the world—," Kant begins, "can possibly be conceived which
could be called good without qualification except a *good will*." To
begin like that is precisely to begin with morality, for it is only
the agent's faculty for initiating action—that being what the will
is—which is good in itself. All other possible goods, the actions
themselves, talents, acquisitions, circumstances, or, above all,
the end to be achieved, are only conditionally or relatively good,
since they might all be in certain situations, productive of harm.
I want to say in passing that it is a very deep assumption that
only the will and never its object can be simply good.

At any rate, the will is clearly the central notion of morality. The perfectly good will, which Kant calls a *holy* will, is one
which always obeys its own "ought." Human beings do *not*

always do as they know they ought. That is Kant's *second* moral fact. The first was that we all experience an inner obligation to certain actions; the second is that we by no means always discharge it. Kant never confuses, as he is sometimes accused of doing, the universality of the moral command with the frequency of its execution.

When the kind of being that knows an "ought" but does not, from merely knowing it, necessarily obey it—when such a being does do as it ought, it is said to be doing its *duty*. Duty is the morality of beings whose will is handicapped. "The concept of duty," Kant says, ". . . contains that of a good will though with certain restrictions and hindrances." When, however, such a being, a *human* being, *can* be said to do its duty, it must do so from no ulterior motive but out of mere respect for its own inner voice, not *from incentive* of reward, nor *by compulsion* of command, but *for the sake* of the law.

Here I must go outside of the *Foundations* to deal with two related matters: the reason why Kant founds his philosophy on the good will rather than on an objective good, and what it means to be a human being, a being with a defective will.

This necessary tangent requires me to set out in the briefest way Kant's system as reflected in the major texts. You know that the central works are all called "critiques": There is a *Critique of Pure Reason*, a *Critique of Practical Reason*, and a third critique I shall barely mention at the end of the lecture. The word "critique" is used by Kant for an inquiry into the *grounds* of human knowledge, and that means for him, into the human faculties. The purpose of each critique is to *certify* some knowledge or activity which is already ours, to give us certain guarantees of its possibility—the desire for *certainty* is the guiding motive of Kant's enterprise.

The *Critique of Pure Reason* inquires into the faculty of experiential knowledge; it grounds what for Kant is the sole material knowledge we can have, the *science of nature*. The second critique gives the grounds of moral action for which the term "practical" is reserved; later we shall see why.

Each of these texts is preceded by a short preliminary work which analyzes respectively the established natural science and the common moral experience to discover what faculties we must possess to make them possible. The *Foundations of the Metaphysics of Morals*, the work we are at this moment studying, is one of these; it was actually published three years before its critique, in 1785. The critique itself is named from the faculty which is disclosed in the last section of the *Foundation*, the "practical reason," of course. (Just for the sake of systematic completeness, I might mention here that both critiques are followed by works giving the actual metaphysical systems grounded in the faculties, namely the *Metaphysical Foundations of Natural Science* and the *Metaphysics of Morals*.)

The main point of this sketch of Kant's works is to document their all-determining, fundamental division into theoretical and practical philosophy. To quote from the first critique: "The law-giving of human reason (*i.e.* philosophy) has two objects, Nature and Freedom, and thus contains both the law of nature and the law of morality, initially in two separate, but eventually in one philosophical system."

Now I think that the practical reason may be the centerpiece of Kant's philosophy, but that it is circumscribed and negatively defined, silhouetted, so to speak, by the pure reason, its backstay. Morality begins where nature ends. So I must try to do the impossible and supply a three-minute review of the *Critique of Pure Reason*, which contains the account of nature.

The account of *nature* and the account of the *science of nature* are for Kant identical. That is because the system of nature is determined by the way our *Sensibility* forms and our *Understanding* functions over the sensations that come to us. This Understanding is a sub-faculty of the Reason, and its function is the structuring of appearances so as to unify them into a lawful system of *things*, the system of nature and natural laws. What is relevant to my exposition is that, while we ourselves are the legislators who constitute nature, we are *not* so freely and consciously; our understanding does its regulating, as it were, behind our backs; we cannot alter or abrogate its dispositions.

What is more, we ourselves are a part of rule-bound nature. For nature consists of ordered *external* appearances, the *physical* appearances of space, but also of *inner* appearances, the *psychological* events of our temporal consciousness. So, as human beings, we are at least partly of a piece with nature. Our behavior is controlled by inexorable psychic mechanisms, akin to the laws of nature in being invariable sequences of cause and effect. Our desires and inclinations are as tendencies to motion, psychic lunges, incited by an *object* of desire or fear, as bodies are attracted or repelled by other bodies; we go after our natural ends not because of their intrinsic worth, but because they push or pull and bend us systematically—by *inclination*, as Kant says, using a physical term. Consequently, Kant has a most melancholy understanding of happiness: It is simply the—ever elusive—sum total of achieved desire, the successful completion of all psychic motion. (Let me, incidentally, remind you that this theory of happiness was set out within a decade of the Declaration of Independence and its inalienable human right to the "pursuit of happiness," a pursuit which has been understood as a similarly infinite chase.)

As natural beings we are, then, in Kant's term, "pathological," meaning that we suffer rather than act, that we are passive rather than "practical." (Kant uses the word *practical* to signify a willed action, a *deed* as opposed to mere behavior.)

Now we can see why our morality is a morality of duty. The *Will*, our power of initiating action, is defined by Kant as a faculty for causing the reality of objects through ideas, that is to say, a faculty for realizing our conceptions. But our conceived object is naturally the object of a wish or a desire. Yet by a desire, as I have just pointed out, we are but passively drawn; our motion toward its object is but a pseudo-action, not a genuine exercise of the Will. (Kant has a special word for such an object-determined choice: *Willkür*, usually rendered in English "will" with a lower case *w*.) Aristotle says in the *Ethics*: "If anyone says that the pleasant or the beautiful exercise compulsion on the ground that they are external to us and compel us, we must answer that this would make everything compulsory, seeing that we do everything we do for their sake." Kant wants to say just that, namely, that all motion after external goods is compulsive, but he also wants to assert that we do *not* do everything for the sake of an external object.

He proceeds, in sum, by conceiving human beings as rational *and* natural beings, as double beings with a double will, a pathologically affected faculty of choice as well as a practical faculty for initiating action. This latter, pure Will, is led by no external purpose, aim, or object, but only by its very own laws and ends.

Therefore, to act from duty is to follow the internal command, the Ought of the pure Will, and to resist the pull of desire. Duty is, to begin with, to be *negatively* apprehended as resistance to the mechanisms of nature. We can never experience ourselves as doing as we ought except when we deny ourselves as natural beings, for only nature has sensible appearances and can be experienced, and we can *feel* the Will only as *thwarted happiness*. That is by no means to say that morality *lies* in opposing our natural inclination—only that its sole evidence is of this negative sort. All we can know of our willing is that we are *capable* of doing our duty. But how can we know even that?

Here, halfway through the exploration, let me recapitulate. We saw what a categorical imperative in general was, namely an unconditional command so formulated as to be capable of adoption by any rational being. Next we saw that Kant's moral philosophy is a philosophy of intention, and begins with the moral fact of the sense of duty, an internal command of the Will; furthermore morality takes the form of duty for those rational beings who have a will whose agency is sometimes blocked by the mechanism of their nature, namely the pull of desire. Finally we saw that human beings are beings of just that kind, for whom to will means to come into conflict with the natural self.

What remains to be articulated is the *positive* aspect of morality. How is it that we nonetheless believe ourselves able to exert our Will freely? And what actually is the command it issues? That, after all, comes near the problem with which we began: Does the moral law, which, as we have seen, appears as the Ought of duty, have the form of a categorical imperative?

Now is the moment to draw together the two terms, Will and Reason. The Will, Kant repeatedly reveals, is nothing but the Reason in its practical capacity. It is not merely associated with rationality; it *is* reason. Note that this identification is another crucial juncture, a taproot of the system. Will is reason initiating action, or, as Kant says, *determining* itself to action: By being "determined" is meant being pulled together out of the laxness of abeyance to become a springboard for specific deeds. Recall that the subfaculty of reason called the understanding constitutes and consequently knows nature and that therefore natural science is certain. The upper reason, however, Reason proper, has *no* object of knowledge; the critique of pure reason is, among other things, a criticism of the unwarranted uses of reason as a faculty of knowledge. Instead it is a *power of action*, a practical faculty. The understanding regulates appearances, but unconsciously; the practical reason, on the other hand, consciously legislates. To make laws for itself is, as we have seen, for Kant the very essence of reason and to enforce them its very life. Reason is self-controlled, self-determined, self-legislating. It is *autonomous*: the word means simply "self-legislating."

Such autonomy is what Kant calls *Freedom*. We have a free will; we can obey the command of duty because it is our innermost, supersensible self that issues it.

The idea of freedom and the will as a faculty of freedom are discovered as necessarily implied by the fact of morality in the third and last section of the *Foundations*. Note that I am holding the great middle section in abeyance for the moment.

What, then, is freedom? Negatively it is what is *not* nature—a mystery, namely a non-natural causality, an invisible, supersensible source of change in the time- and space-bound sensible natural sequences and connections, the occasion of natural motions with supernatural significance.

Positively, freedom is nothing but that very autonomy, that power of being a law unto itself, which characterizes the practical reason. What makes freedom possible is beyond all knowing, but what makes the moral law possible—that is to say, what makes it possible to obey the moral law—is freedom itself. The fact that we have a faculty of freedom is the critical ground of the possibility of morality. The moral law is in need of such grounding because, while a mere *analysis* of the concept of desires will inform us that we *will* follow them, nothing in the mere concept of a moral law tells us that we *can* obey it. It therefore needs a ground on which the command form "You ought!" is effectively conjoined to the thing to be done. (Incidentally, Kant calls such a proposition, in which terms are conjoined on grounds other than their mere meaning, a *synthetic* proposition, and when it is given from beyond experience, he calls it a synthetic *a priori* proposition.)

Morality, therefore, demands freedom, and freedom grounds morality. We can now collect all the chief terms of Kant's moral discourse: Freedom is the radical power of the Reason to become practical, to determine itself as a Will, a supersensible cause of natural events. The human being is a rational being that can, however, appear to itself only as a part of nature. Therefore it apprehends the rulings of its will as an "Ought," as a command to do its duty in the face of the compelling mechanisms of its nature. The injunction of its Will is the moral law.

That law, being laid down by reason for reason, must have the form of rationality. It is therefore an *imperative*. Furthermore, it must command an action in no way contingent on external circumstance. It is therefore a *categorical* imperative. Finally, it must as a law of reason have the mark of universality, of covering all cases, and hence it must be unique. It is therefore *the* Categorical Imperative.

And now, at last, I return to the middle section where it is actually formulated in three main versions. The first formulation is:

Act only according to that maxim by which you can at the same time will that it should become a universal law.

Let us see what this formula contains. It contains a new term, "maxim." A *maxim* is my private, individual, "subjective" reason for a choice. It is intelligible enough, but it is individual in being contingent on my desires. A maxim is whatever subjective reason articulate beings give themselves for acting.

Now the imperative says precisely that those private reasons must be regulated. It says that they must always be required to have the character of a law of Reason. They must not be merely subjective but must be capable of being universalized. The Categorical Imperative commands only this: that every action should be performed for a reason having the character of a law. It does not command this or that particular action. It does not even lay down this or that specific law. It only requires *lawfulness itself*. The first version of the moral law simply requires the will to act *as* a Will, namely in accordance with its character as Practical Reason.

Let me right here forestall what seems to me to be a niggling, logic-chopping objection to this grand rule. It is said that anyone can undercut its authority by so particularly specifying a maxim that the class of actions to which it applies contains only his own, and its universalization is emptily guaranteed. For example, I can take the maxim that I, standing at precisely my co-ordinates at precisely the present moment, may tell you lies. The universalized version of this maxim will then say that *anyone* in my precise position may tell lies, there being, however, no one else in that class. But of course, Kant intends no such craftiness. The working import of his severe and noble rule is plain enough: Never take the easy way; never make an exception of yourself! The illustrative cases he immediately furnishes make that perfectly clear.

Another immediate criticism, derived precisely from a loose reading of one of these cases, is a simple mistake. Kant says that a maxim may fail to be a fit rule of moral action for one of two reasons. The first is because its universalization is self-contradictory: If I lie, and so all may lie, speech itself, the instrument with which I meant to deceive, is destroyed. The second is because the universalization is clearly undesirable: If I will not aid others, they need not aid me. Now it has been argued from the latter example that Kant's morality is after all enmeshed in a calculus of convenience and desire. But the desire for help from others is *not* the reason why we ourselves must not adopt a maxim of selfishness. The reason for rejecting that maxim follows from the pure formalism of the Categorical Imperative: It is that we cannot *reasonably universalize* such a maxim, whether we ourselves will ever need help or not.

Clearly, the major problem connected with this version of the imperative arises from the framing of maxims and the testing of universalizations. I shall return to it at the very end.

Let me now go to the second version. It says:

Act so as to treat humanity, whether in your own person or in that of another, always as an end and never as a means only.

It is almost unnecessary to remark that however repellently severe Kant's moral law may seem, this version at least goes straight to our republican hearts. The reason is plain: It is clearly the rule which gives the moral basis of our own political disposition, our democratic way of life, which requires that we accord others the respect belonging to self-determined beings capable of making their own decisions for themselves, and that when we use them, as Kant knows we sometimes must, we do not *only* use them. Indeed, in the aforementioned sequel to the critical inquiry, the *Metaphysics of Morals*, justice, the principle which binds human beings into a political system, is directly derived from this version: Justice is so dealing with others as to make my freedom compatible with theirs.

For that is precisely what it means to regard others as ends in themselves. It means considering them not as things but as persons, not as the means to our happiness, but as, in their turn, independent, ultimate law-givers, free beings whose Will consults no end but its own. That is also precisely how Kant connects the first and the second formula. And that is where trouble starts.

For, to begin with, there is in the Kantian system no external appearance by which to recognize a fellow will in its interiority. One may only conjecture that some exemplar of the natural species *homo sapiens* is in fact a rational being. But let that deep problem of intersubjective recognition be. What is more immediately to the point is this question: Why *should* I, and further, how *could* I, take another free being as an end? For that it is an end in itself cannot logically make it an end for me. Furthermore, its very worth lies in the performance of its duty even to the point of thwarting its own happiness; what sense does it make for me to meddle with its external well-being, which plays no part in its self-sufficiency? (You may immediately be reminded of a problem in political morality that is always with us, namely how to minister to the welfare of human beings while preserving their self-determination.) The most appealing version of the Categorical Imperative is also the most shaky in its systematic derivation.

Let me do no more than read the third version, because you will see right away that it is nothing but the sum and substance, plainly stated, of all that has gone before. Significantly, it is not even framed as an imperative, but simply as a condition, the condition that the Will must harmonize with universal practical reason, as an idea to be held in every moral person's mind, namely:

> The idea of the Will of every rational being as making universal law.

It is the ultimate formulation of Kant's Moral Law.

I invite you to consider how remarkable it is that a principle so formal, so empty of specific content, gives rise to so characteristic a morality. Indeed, all the criticisms accusing it of excessive formalism or excessive flexibility seem to me miscon-structions. Kantian morality issues in concrete kinds of conduct and definitely predictable deeds: uncompromising adher-ence to principle; the exclusion of any sentimentality from the effort to do good; unwillingness to let circumstances, private or social, lift responsibility for his deeds from the individual. Accordingly literature, especially German literature, abounds in vividly severe Kantian characters who perform their duty in the face of their natural humanity; they are evidently drawn from life, especially from the Prussian military and officialdom whose harsh virtues came from a Kantian training, for exam-ple, Baron Innstetten in Theodor Fontane's *Effi Briest*.

Therefore, the most telling criticisms of Kant's moral phi-losophy have to be dredged up, it seems to me, from the sub-structure of the system itself. Although I must be very brief, I do want to run through some of those difficulties, because, as I mentioned in the beginning, this sort of critical rooting-about in a system is not the worst way to work one's way into it. Besides, you have probably already formed suspicions of your own which I might help you articulate.

Clearly all the difficulties begin with Kant's idea of rea-son itself as a law-giving function. (There are, of course, other conceptions of the intellect, for instance as a *receptive* capabil-ity—such a conception precludes, to be sure, epistemological guarantees of certainty.) Hand in hand with the radical self-determination of Kantian reason goes the pathological mech-anism of the temporal consciousness, a sharp opposition of freedom and nature that disallows in *principle* the possibility of any object of desire which is also good in itself, and so fore-stalls the very inquiry of greatest interest to most of us.

Again bound up with the uncompromisingly mechanistic view of desire is Kant's repellent view of happiness as the un-attainable satisfaction of all desires. Now that conception is be-lied by any moment of real happiness we have ever had, not only by the fact that we *have* attained it, but also by its qual-ity: fulfilled desire is not what happiness feels like. Besides, in being quite disconnected from the performance of duty, such happiness is related to moral goodness only through the *worthiness* to be happy and the cold comfort of that strange exception to the strict separation of reason and the emotions which Kant has contrived, the moral feeling of self-respect. (Kant's guarantor, by the way, of an ultimate concurrence of moral worthiness and pathological happiness is a mere hypothesis, a god posited to serve just this function.) But some direct connection between acting well and living well seems to me to be both required and indicated by human experience. Virtue is the realization of morality in a living disposition, and therefore the notion of Kantian virtue will display the quandary in the disconnection of morality from the good life. For, just as one might expect in view of the stern demands of Kantian morality, human virtue is presented in its place, the *Metaphysics of Morals*, as essentially *fortitude*, strength of character acquired by rigorous ethical training. But what possible role can such an acquired, *habitual* disposition of the phenomenal consciousness play, when the Categorical Imperative requires precisely a radically *rational* response to every case? Indeed, one would think that there could be no direct, positive, persisting external structure of Kantian morality, no visible and exemplary virtue—no such thing as the firmly and finely moulded moral excellence of antiquity. The Kantian man of duty does, to be sure, bear the strong stamp of his morality in his respectability, but that is the consequence and not the source of his deeds. The emphasis on the continuously radical agency of the will shapes moral life as a succession of knife-edge decisions and of crucial moments in which our self-respect is forever in the balance. It seems to me that there *are* such moral moments, when all comfortable contexts, all decent habits fail and our naked integrity is at stake. For such crises the Categorical Imperative is made, but not for the continuous stream of reasonable life which it seems to me that a moral science ought to shape.

Instead of a conclusion let me end with a coda of a slightly technical but also of a consolidating sort. Almost by the way, and not counting it among the standard versions of the Categorical Imperative, Kant offers the following formulation:

Act as though the maxim of your actions were by your Will to become a law of nature.

The formula appears in the *Critique of Practical Reason* with much more emphasis under the title of "Typic of pure practical judgment." It is essentially a rule of instruction for forming maxims, or rather for testing maxims to see if they can be made into universal laws. In sum, it is the founding rule for the—very necessary—moral science of maxim-making. For obviously, to do as I ought, I must, albeit incidentally, also know *what* to do; the "So act" must have a content. Thus we see that although for Kant virtue is not knowledge, yet the decisions of the practical reason are imbedded in the judgments of pure reason. We must *know* a criterion for deciding what maxims bear universalization.

Such a criterion, the formula informs us, is to be derived from the science of nature. We must know nature's works, its interactions and reciprocities, its harmonies and balances well enough to be able to make a speculative projection of our maxims, and to imagine what the world would be like if the contemplated choice occurred inevitably, mechanistically and universally, as a law of nature. What, for instance, would a world governed by a maxim of selfishness look like, a world deterministically devoid of benevolence—a question which we require a certain experience of nature to answer. Thus, as Kant had promised, there is a rapprochement of the science of nature and what he calls the "casuistry" of morality. And that was to be expected.

For first, we ourselves are, through the structuring functions of our understanding, the makers, and immediately also the knowers, of nature. Yet the rules of our understanding, the faculty which structures appearance in its basic reality, do not determine *particular* occurrences, but only the general system of things and their relations, which is precisely what Kant calls nature. That indeterminacy enables us, as knowers of nature, to turn her to our own purposes, to move mountains and manipulate people. Such acts of applied science are performed according to what Kant calls a technical or a *hypothetical* imperative, which is the very contrary of a categorical imperative, since it always has the form: "*If* you *desire* such and such a result, do such and such because it is technically or prudentially appropriate." If you would level a hill, lay a charge of dynamite; if you would win a crowd, promise things.

Such technical interferences with nature are certainly phenomenal, in both senses—apparent and sometimes spectacular. They appear because they are, after all, but the interaction of inner psychic and outer physical nature; they are not *deeds* of practical reason. Moral action, on the other hand, is a true irruption of rational purpose into the course of natural events. It is a second law-giving which grafts upon nature a second, an invisible order which is yet of the "type" of a natural law—a system of harmonious *lawfulness*. The act of nature-making which the understanding accomplishes *automatically* is to be consummated by practical reason *consciously*. But the effects of the free will can never be evident as such: however our moral purpose may re-route nature, what appears will still be the course of nature. First and last, there can be no phenomenal morality.

And yet there is at least a visible *symbol* of the possible unity of the two law-givings. It is an appearance which stands for the *possible* harmony of natural and moral lawfulness. Kant introduces it in the last critique, the *Critique of Judgment*. It is *the beautiful*. For beauty raises in us a pleasure, which is without desire, at the harmonious interplay of our free sensual imagination and the lawful nature produced by our understanding. Therefore a thing of beauty is analogous to a moral deed which our free will, without regard to inclination, must work in the world of determined nature. So, although beauty is *only* a symbol, it is yet a source of hope for the possibility of effective obedience to Kant's Imperative and for its product: a morally informed nature.

5

KANT'S PHILOSOPHICAL USE OF MATHEMATICS

NEGATIVE MAGNITUDES

I HOPE THAT THIS consideration of a peculiar little work of great interest by Kant will do honor and give pleasure to my friend Stanley Rosen. The text is an essay called "An Attempt to Introduce the Concept of Negative Magnitudes into Philosophy (*Weltweisheit*)." Its date is 1763.

Its appeal to me has these three aspects: First there is the tentative mode expressed in the title; here we hear Kant's pre-critical voice—not yet the magisterially conclusive notes of the *Critique of Pure Reason* (1781) but a tone at once spiritedly daring and gropingly uncertain. A second and more specific aspect is the inchoate appearance of major elements of the first *Critique*;

This essay was first published in *Logos and Eros: Essays Honoring Stanley Rosen*, ed. Nalin Ranasinghe (St. Augustine's Press, 2006).

we can see its thinking come into being. The third appealing aspect of the essay is its pedagogic suggestiveness; for a teacher seeking to help students reflect on mathematical formalisms, it is a useful source.

The piece on negative magnitudes has been eclipsed by its much longer contemporary, "The Only Possible Basis of Proof for a Demonstration of God's Existence (*Dasein*)," dated 1763. This essay was subjected to an extensive and deep analysis by Heidegger in his lecture course of 1927 (*The Problems of Phenomenology*, trans. and ed. Albert Hofstadter, Indiana Univ. Press, 1982, ¶ 8); his elucidation of Kant's use of the term "reality" is particularly relevant to the essay on negative magnitudes.

What evidently drew Heidegger's attention to this essay, however, was its brisk definition of *Dasein*—his central word— as "absolute position." When the verb "is" is used not as a copula to relate a subject to its predicate as in "God is omnipotent" but is asserted abruptly, *absolutely*, as in "God is" or "God exists," it signifies, Kant claims, a mere *positing* of an object. By this, in Heidegger's interpretation, Kant means that the object is affirmed by a *knowing subject* as available to *perception*. (I observe, incidentally, that in order to express the character of existence as non-attributive absolute position more adequately, Kant proposes language that anticipates the existential quantifier of propositional logic: We should say not "A narwhal is an animal" but "A narwhal is an animal with unicorn attributes.") In other words, existence is not a predicate and adds no objective attribute to God's essence. Since it is the crux of what Kant first called the ontological argument (whose best known proponent is Anselm) that existence is a necessary attribute of God's essence, Kant's understanding of existence as a non-predicate seems to be a refutation of that proof.

Kant's own demonstration calls on the concept of a "realground" (*Realgrund*) that emerges in the essay on negative magnitudes, to be discussed below. This concept in turn involves the postulate that essence is prior to existence and actuality to possibility. Since Heidegger's thinking is dominated by the reverse claim, he is a severe if respectful critic of Kant's understanding. He regards Kant's exposition of existence as a halfway house, situated between the notion of existence as one predicate among others and his own understanding of *Dasein* as "extantness," i.e. "being-at-hand," with respect to things and "being in the world" with respect to human beings.

There is yet another contemporary essay that has bearing on the essay about negative magnitudes, the "Enquiry Concerning the Evidence of the Principles of Natural Theology and Morality, in Answer to a Question Posed by the Royal Academy of the Sciences at Berlin for 1763." The aim of this essay (which did not win the prize) was to establish what evidence and certainty natural theology is capable of; it is thus a discourse on method. It begins with an investigation of the difference between mathematics and metaphysics (a difference that plays a major role even in Kant's last work, the *Opus Postumum*).

Thus both pieces, the one on God's existence and the other on theological certainty, illuminate the essay on negative magnitudes, the former through its concept of an ultimate reality and the latter through its restrictions on the use of mathematics in first philosophy. I will draw on them in my exploration.

ANYONE WHO HAS STEPPED OUT for a moment from the routine familiarity of operations with signed numbers will have wondered just how, say, 5, +5, |5| differ from each other, and, furthermore, whether +5 and −5 are operations on or qualifications of the number 5. Although his essay concerns numerable magnitudes, especially those discovered in nature, questions of that sort seem to have been going through Kant's mind, as he considered the illuminations that the actual quantification of experience might offer to philosophy.

In the essay on natural theology Kant sets out four definitive reasons why the mathematical *method* is inapplicable to philosophy and is not the way to certainty in metaphysics (¶ 1–4):

1. Mathematical definitions are "synthetic," in the sense that the mathematician does not analyze a given concept, but

first synthesizes or constructs it, i.e., puts it together at will. (In the first *Critique* synthesis will have acquired a deeper meaning; it will no longer mean arbitrary construction but an act of the understanding expressing in the imagination the formative givens of the intuition.) In philosophy or, as Kant says interchangeably, *Weltweisheit*, "world-wisdom" (as distinguished from the scholastic philosophy of mere, unapplied concepts, see *Logic*, Intro. III), on the other hand, definitions are analytic, in the sense that concepts are given to, not made by, the philosopher, and he then endeavors to analyze them into their implicit elements. (In the *Critique* a way will be found for the philosopher too to form pure synthetic judgments.)

2. Mathematics is always concrete, in that the arithmetician symbolizes his numbers and operations perceptibly, and the geometer visibly draws his figures. (In the *Critique* these inscriptions will be within the field of the imaginative intuition.) Philosophers, on the other hand, use words exclusively, and these signify, in Kant's understanding, abstractly, non-pictorially. (In the *Critique* this rift between word and picture is closed.)

3. The mathematician tries to employ a minimum of unproved propositions (i.e., axioms and postulates), while the philosopher makes indefinitely many assumptions, as needed. (In the *Critique* the principles of experience will be systematically restricted.)

4. The objects of mathematics are easy and simple (!), those of philosophy difficult and involved.

In the *Preface* of "The Attempt to Introduce the Concept of Negative Magnitudes into Philosophy" Kant accordingly eschews the introduction of mathematical *method* into philosophy, but censures the neglect of the application of mathematical *matter* to the objects of philosophy. The really useful mathematical doctrines are, however, only those that are applicable to natural science. (This restriction prefigures the use of mathematics in the *Critique*, where its role is the constitution and understanding of the system of nature, i.e., of matter in quantitative and qualitative change.) As a preliminary example, Kant gives the continuity of space, which is, if inexplicitly, postulated in the Euclidean geometry he assumes. The concept of continuity will give insight, he thinks (but explains no further), into the ultimate ground of the possibility of space. (The claim does prefigure the arguments for the establishment of a spatial intuition in the *Critique*.) The main example in this piece will, of course, be the concept of negative magnitudes, which Kant now proceeds to clarify and apply. I shall follow his arguments through the three sections of the essay.

FIRST SECTION

There are two types of opposition: *logical*, through contradiction, and *real*, without contradiction. If contradictories are logically connected, the result is a "negative nothing, an unthinkable" (*nihil negativum irrepresentabile*; now as later in the *Critique*, *representabile* = *cogitabile*, i.e., to think is to represent in the cognitive faculty). Thus a body in motion is a "something" (which is in the *Critique* the highest objective concept, i.e., that of an object in general); so is a body at rest. But a body at the same time in motion and at rest is an unthinkable nothing. It is not so much a non-object incapable of being as a less-than-nothing incapable of being thought.

Real-opposition (*Realentgegensetzung*), on the other hand, involves no contradiction and thus no unthinkability. For this opposition does not cancel the being of the object thus qualified; it remains a something and thinkable (*cogitabile*). Suppose a body impelled in one direction and also driven by a counterforce in the other. The resulting motion may be none = 0, but the body so affected is not a no-thing. Kant calls this result *nihil privativum representabile*, where *privativum* has a dynamic sense, as of an achieved condition. This nothing is to be termed zero = 0.

Kant also refers to real-opposition as real-repugnance (*Realrepugnanz*) because two precisely antagonistic predicates of an object cancel each other, though they do not annihilate the object they qualify. Moreover, it is somewhat arbitrary (or rather, determined by extraneous human interests) which pole is called negative. For example, "dark" may seem to us intrinsically negative, but it is canceled by its own negation "not-dark" (which might, of course, actually be light). Thus one may say that in real-repugnance both opposing predicates are affirmative.

Kant gives, among others, the following example. Suppose a person owes 100 dollars and is, at the same time, owed this sum. This debtor-lender is worth 0 dollars, since the two conditions cancel each other, but this fact does not cancel *him*, the bearer of these modifications.

Kant then offers an example (slightly adjusted by me) which expands the concept of real-opposition. Suppose a vessel going from Portugal to Brazil is carried due west by an east wind with an impelling force that would cause it to run 12 miles on a certain day, and is also subject to a countervailing current retarding it by 5 miles; the boat's total progress is seven miles a day. Here the result is not = 0. It is clear that Kant regards real-opposition as taking place along a scaled spectrum of quantifiable qualities at whose center there might be (though there is not always) a neutral fulcrum, 0.

If there *is* an "origin," then on one side there are the positive quantities, on the other those that can be regarded either as the relative negatives of the former, or as opposed positives in their own right. Thus the opening question, what is really meant by +5, −5 and |5|, *might* be answered by Kant like this: The plus or minus sign is neither an implicit operation nor a qualification of the number as itself inherently positive or negative, for the number is, like its "absolute" expression |5|, always positive. The plus and minus signs signify rather the *relation of numbers to each other*: −5 is the negative of +5; it is negative only in relation to a positive five. To be sure, since Kant is not speaking of bare numbers but of magnitudes symbolizing quantified properties such as are representable along one dimension, being in real-opposition, the application to pure numbers is conjectural.

Objects in real-opposition have, of course, many negations besides those directly opposing a positive: a ship sailing westward is also not sailing southward, but its course is in real-opposition only to the eastern direction. Moreover, there are cases, say of lack of motion, which are not the result of real opposing forces but of a total absence of impelling force. Negation that is the result of real-opposition Kant calls *privatio*, that which has no positive ground is called *defectus* or *absentia*. His example of an absent or null result is what we would call potential energy (not to be confused with "potential-opposition," see below): "Thus the thunder that art discovered for the sake of destruction lies stored up for a future war in the threatening silence of an arsenal of a prince, until, when a treacherous tinder touches it, it blows up like lightning and devastates everything around it." Aside from Kant's pacifistic poetry, this example shows that Kant is considering only the magnitudes of *actualized* forces.

It is pretty clear that what Kant is struggling to do is to present a conceptual underpinning for what we call directed magnitudes as they occur in the world, including signed numbers insofar as they represent natural qualities, whose plus or minus tells us whether we are to move respectively to the right or the left along the line-spectrum (conceived as a straight line, where left is negative by convention). Not that Kant is thinking of our mathematical number line.—He does not even mention an origin (=0), and his opposition-spectra are evidently not necessarily infinite in either direction. While he does insist on the relative directionality of negative numbers, insofar as they countermand their positives, he also reiterates that the negatively directed magnitudes are *not* negative numbers if these are regarded as being less than 0.

For the use of directed magnitudes in philosophy it will in fact be essential that the opposed quantities are indeed inherently positive, as will be shown in Section Three. Hence a debt can be called negative capital, falling negative rising, and so on, where it is our perspective that gives a negative emotional tint to one of the terms. Kant sums it up in a basic law and its converse: 1. Real-repugnance takes place between two positives, power against power, which cannot be contradictories but must be of the same kind (while the complement class in a contradiction, e.g., "non-dark objects," is not necessarily of the "same kind" as "dark objects"; they might be invisible objects). 2. Where a positive opposes its proper positive, a real cancellation will occur.

Furthermore certain rules of operation follow. For example, if the opposites are quantitatively equal, their sum will = 0, or $A - A = 0$, which shows, Kant explains, that both A's are positive (since $A = A$). Also $A + 0 = A$ and $A - 0 = A$, since no oppositions are involved. But $0 - A$ is philosophically impossible since positives cannot be subtracted from nothing: There are no inherently negative qualities and so, as was said, no directed *magnitudes* inherently less than 0 (!). This odd-sounding but unavoidable consequence will have important metaphysical implications.

Real-repugnance, strange though its label be, has an Aristotelian antecedent. It is, I want to argue, a dynamic version of the logical opposition Aristotle calls *contrariety* (*Metaphysics* X, 4). Kant himself says as much in his *Anthropology* of 1798; he there contrasts contradiction or logical opposition (*Gegenteil*) with *contrariety* or real-opposition (*Widerspiel*, ¶ 60).

As a formal logical opposition contrariety occurs in the Square of Opposition, which is a tabulation of the Aristotelian doctrine on the subject: If the basic proposition is "Every S is P," its contradictory is "Some S is not P" and its contrary is "No S is P." Contradictories cannot both be true nor can they both be false, but contraries, though they cannot both be true, *can* both be false; for if not every S be P, yet might it be false that no S is P. Contrary propositions bear a certain formal relation to contrary *terms*, for these cannot both at once belong to an object but they might both fail to belong to it. Thus an object could not be at once pitch black and pure white, but it needn't be either, which is untrue of contradictories, such as black and not-black.

The above paragraph is really a digression to show that it is not contrary propositions but contrary terms denoting qualities that are related to Kant's real-opposition. Contraries are qualities which are not simply in abrupt polar opposition (though their extremes delimit a maximum difference) but are connected through a spectrum of gradations. Aristotle makes privation a particular case of contrariety, and for Kant negation, interpreted as *privatio* (in German *Beraubung*), "deprivation," introduces into some of the ranges of opposition a kind of null point or zero through which the quality goes by degrees into a negative or oppositional mode. (As was noted, not all the spectra have such a center; for example, when bodies are brought to rest = 0 by countervailing forces this 0 is not an origin in the spectrum of forces but is a net effect in the bodies' position, measured in spatial extension rather than as qualitative intensity.) Some of Kant's examples will be given below.

What turns contrariety into real-repugnance is the dynamic view Kant takes of this opposition: It means not just being supinely, matter-of-factly opposed; it means being antagonistically, aggressively opposed. Moreover, this striving in many different dimensions of quality is quantifiable in degrees of intensity, as Kant's examples will show.

SECOND SECTION

Kant now calls for examples from 1. physics, 2. psychology, 3. morality.

1. In physics his prime example is impenetrability, which is a positive force, a true repulsion that might thus also be called "negative attraction." For attraction is a cause, contrarily directed, by which a body compels others to push into its own space.

2. From psychology (*Seelenlehre*) come Kant's most pungent examples of real-opposition. He raises the question whether

aversion could be called "negative pleasure." The fact that in German aversion, *Unlust*, looks like a direct contradictory of pleasure, *Lust*, gives him pause, but he observes that in "real-understanding" (*Realverstand*), meaning in actual psychic perception, aversion is not just a negation of desire or even its diminution, but a real-repugnance, a positive perception. Then, to illustrate, comes an almost comical quantification: A Spartan mother hears of her son's heroism; a high degree of pleasure ensues, say of 4 degrees. Then comes the news of his death. If the resulting *Unlust* were a mere negation it would equal 0, but $4 + 0 = 4$, as if the death made no difference to her delight. Kant concedes, however (some notion of a mother's feeling!), that the positive *Unlust* of his death, the real-repugnance, will diminish the mother's *Lust* at her son's bravery by one degree, which will therefore $= 3$.

In the same vein, disgust is negative desire, hate negative love, ugliness negative beauty, error negative truth, and so on. Kant warns against regarding this terminology as mere word-mongering: It is a philosophical pitfall to regard the evils of positive privation as mere defects. Thus Kant is denying, surely quite incidentally, the theological doctrine (found in Plotinus, Augustine, Thomas) of evil as privation of good (*privatio boni*), for in Kant's view in this essay evil, though a relative negation, is yet a positive force.

3. Kant naturally regards his concept of real-opposition as having important uses in "practical prudence" (*Weltweisheit*), that is, applied morality. Non-virtue (*Untugend*) is, in human beings, not a mere denial of virtue (*Tugend*), but a positively negative virtue, vice. This is the case because humans, unlike animals which are morally unendowed, have an "inner moral feeling" that drives them to good actions. For instance, they harbor a law of neighborly love. To do bad deeds, human beings have to overcome this natural inclination to good. (A quarter century later, in the second *Critique*, the *Critique of Practical Reason*, 1788, Kant will, on the contrary, see the test of true morality in the overcoming of natural inclinations.)

Thus certain people must make a noticeable effort to engage even in sins of omission (such as neglecting to offer neighborly help), which differ from sins of commission (hurting one's neighbor) only in degree; hence the slide from the one to the other is all too smooth, though the beginning is effortful.

Kant apologizes for what may seem to enlightened readers the prolixity of his exposition. He is writing for an "indocile breed of judges, which, because they spend their lives with a single book, understand nothing but what is contained therein." The book is, I imagine, the Bible.

In an appended Remark, Kant forestalls the notion that the world conceived in such a dynamic balance is capable neither of augmentation nor perfection. He points out 1. that in potential oppositions (to be explained below) though the total quantity of effect may = 0, yet there may be an increase in apparent change, as when bodies widen the distance between them; 2. that it is the very antagonism of natural forces that keeps the world in its perfectly regular courses; and 3. that though desire and aversion do balance each other considered as positive quantities oppositely signed, who would claim that aversion is to be called a perfection? Moreover, though the net quantity of moral action in two people may be the same, yet the quality of the one who acted from the better intention is to be more greatly valued. Kant adds that these calculi don't apply to the godhead which is blessed not through an external good but through itself.

THIRD SECTION

Kant introduces this section, which contains his startling application of the concept of real-opposition to metaphysics, by insisting once more that it is a mere attempt, very imperfect though promising: It is better to put before the public uncertain essays than dogmatically decked-out pretenses of profundity. This section is accordingly called "Containing Some Reflections Which Can Be Preparatory for the Application of the Concept Here Thought Out to the Objects of Philosophy." I dwell on this language because it is not a tone familiar to those of us who have spent time with the three *Critiques*.

Everyone easily understands how it is that something *is not*—the positive ground for its being is absent; there is no reason for it to be. But how does something *cease* to be? The question arises because we must understand every passing-away as a negative becoming. As such it requires a real or positive ground.

In the first two sections Kant had spoken of real-opposition or real-repugnance, by which were meant normally apprehensible contrarieties. Now, in the third section, he introduces real-grounds (*Realgründe*). As far as I can make out from the examples, real-grounds are natural, including psychic, causes: forces, powers, and acts exercised by material or psychic agents. "Real" here is used not as in real-opposition, which is opposed to logical contradiction, but it seems to mean "affecting perceptible existence." Real-grounds seem to be a first-level, underlying causal reality, apprehended through its effects. Thus Kant uses "reality"—and, as we shall see, "existence," "being" (*Wesen*), as well as "actuality" (*Wirklichkeit*)—quite loosely in these exploratory essays; Heidegger shows that Kant's later systematic meaning of reality is the "whatness" of a thing, all its possible predicates, its essence, while existence is perceptibility.

Kant's examples are mainly from the soul. It costs real effort to refrain from laughing, to dissipate grief, even to abstract from a manifold representation for the sake of clarity; thus abstraction is negative attention. Even the apparently random succession of thoughts has real grounds which are "hidden in the depths of the mind (*Geist*)," i.e., in what we call the subconscious. Whether the change is in the condition of matter and thus through external causes, or of the mind and thus through inner causes, the necessity for a causal real-opposition remains the same.

Kant is focusing here, it seems to me, on a partial converse to, and a kind of complement of, a question, evidently not asked by the ancients, which is to become a modern preoccupation:

"Why does something exist rather than nothing?" It was first raised as a metaphysical problem with a theological answer by Leibniz ("The Principles of Nature and Grace, Founded on Reason," 1714), and was repeatedly taken up by Heidegger (especially in "What is Metaphysics?," 1949), who treated it as "the basic question of metaphysics," though to be resolved without recourse to theology.

Leibniz asks for a reason, sufficient and ultimate, to account for the *existence* of a universe of things in progress and finds it in God. Kant, on the other hand, asks for an adequate reason why a present condition in the world should *go out of existence* and finds real-opposition as the cause, though an *unexplained* cause which, Kant says at the end of the essay, he has been and will be thinking about and will in the future write about.— This appears to be a harbinger of Critical works not to appear for almost two decades. Meanwhile the metaphysical consequences are exceedingly strange: *The sum total of all real grounds equals zero*, and "the whole of the world is in itself Nothing." More of this below.

Kant says that the theses to be here proposed seem to him "of the most extreme importance." First, however, he distinguishes real-opposition, or as he now calls it, "actual" opposition, from "possible" or "potential" opposition. The latter type of opposites are also each other's negatives, real to be sure, but not, as it happens, in conflict. Thus two forces, each other's opposites, may be driving two bodies in opposite directions: They have the potential to cancel each other's motion but do not actually do so in the given situation. So also one person's desire may be the other's aversion, yet their ability to stymie each other is only a possibility.

Kant then offers the following first general thesis:

In all natural changes of the world their positive sum, insofar as it is estimated by the addition of agreeing (not opposed) positions and the subtraction from one another of those in real-opposition, is neither increased nor diminished.

Recall Newton's Third Law of Motion (*Philophiae Naturalis Principia Mathematica*, 1687):

> To every action there is opposed an equal reaction: or, the mutual actions of two bodies upon each other are always equal, and directed to contrary parts.

It is pretty evident that Kant is struggling to ground in metaphysics and apply to the human world the most dynamic of Newton's Laws of Motion or perhaps the Law of the Conservation of Momentum, which is implied in (or, some argue, implies) the law of equal action and reaction; it states that when the forces acting on bodies in the same and in contrary directions are summed (over time) the quantity of motion (i.e., the mass compounded with velocity = mv) is not changed. Kant says without proof that although this rule of mechanics is not usually deduced from the metaphysical ground from which his first thesis is derived, yet it could be. (The first *Critique* will be partly devoted to giving the transcendental grounds of the laws of motion and conservation.)

Not only bodies in motion but souls in emotion obey the law of conservation, and so do humans in action. Astoundingly, Kant really means this: For every "world-change," i.e., every "natural" change (which includes the psychic realm) there is an equal and opposed change, so that the sum of measured final positions, i.e., states of existence taken globally, is equal to what it was before the change, or the total effect = 0.

Every becoming, then, induces an actual or potential counter-becoming or cessation. It can now be seen why Kant introduced potential real-opposition: Kant's forces not only act in opposed pairs but they may act on *different* objects, i.e., the real-opposition may not be actualized in one body or one soul or even in the same mode in one soul. Nevertheless these potential oppositions enter into the summed effects of the world-total.

Kant then goes on to give more concrete non-mechanical examples—though these are not non-natural, because (as will still be true in the *Critiques*) the soul, excepting in its practical-moral employment of reason, is subject to natural dynamic forces. The examples of this third section differ from the ones in the previous section exactly as the course of the exposition requires: They are cases not of actual but of potential real-opposition. Thus if one person's pleasure and displeasure arise not from the same object, but the same ground that caused pleasure in one object is also the true ground for feeling displeasure in *another*, then in analogy to two bodies moving in contrary directions by repulsion, there is one potential real-ground and cause for the positive and the negative feeling. These feelings oppose but also bypass each other; they may cancel each other but need not do so. This is why the Stoic sage had to eradicate all pleasurable drives—because they always engender an associated but diverse displeasure that affects the final value of the pleasure, though perhaps not the actual pleasure itself. Even in the use of the understanding, we find that to the degree that one idea is clarified, the others may be obscured, though surely not by the clarification. Kant adds that in the most perfect Being the zero sum result does not hold, as will be shown.

Now comes the second thesis, which is simply the translation of the first thesis into its causative grounds:

> All real-grounds of the universe, if one sums those similarly directed and subtracts those opposed to one another, yield a result which is equal to zero.

Kant immediately states: "The whole of the world is in itself nothing, except insofar as it is something through the will of someone other." Regarded by itself, the sum of all existing reality = 0; the world is an almost Heraclitean system of balanced oppositions, of mutually negating positivities. In relation to the divine will the sum of all possible reality, of the world's existence, is, however, positive. But it itself is not therefore in real-opposition to the divine will; it is not the godhead's relative negation. Consequently existence, i.e., whatever is perceptibly there in the world, is through its *internal* relations nothing, but in relation to the grounding will of the divinity it is something; it is positive. For there can be no real-opposition of the world to the divine will. (This thought is still to be found in the *Opus Postumum*.)

The nullity of the physical and psychical world in its summed effects, the nothingness of the underlying universe of summed causes, and the positivity of creation only in relation to God—Kant presents these results without any discernible pathos, without acknowledgment that this cancellation of the world-whole of effect and cause might bear a religious or moral interpretation beyond the intellectual proof of God's existence. Nor can I discover that he ever reverted to this nullifying construal of the laws of conservation. Perhaps it is to be regarded as a passing notion that served as a spur to further inquiry into the world's relation to its ground. (Kant does hold on to the "law of the antagonism in all community of matter by means of motion"; any divergence from its reciprocity would, he now argues, move the very center of gravity of the universe, *Metaphysical Foundations of Natural Science* of 1786, ¶ 563. In this essay too the notion of real-opposition is put to work in the specific antagonism of repulsion and attraction, forces which between them are responsible for the way matter, i.e., "the movable," fills space. However, the explanation of these forces in their specificity remains an unsolved problem for Kant into the *Opus Postumum*.)

So Kant concludes by making *explicit* the heretofore assumed conversion: Because the internal sum of existence is zero, it follows that the "real-grounds," i.e., the forces and powers producing effects in the world, must be in a corresponding opposition: The realm of existing and possible reality is in itself shot through with grounding polarities that cancel existence, though in respect to the divine will (Kant doesn't speak of "God" in this context) it has positive being (*Wesen*). This overt conclusion of the last section is surprising, since it follows close on the assertion that the zero sum of all existence flows necessarily from the grounding being (*Wesen*) of the world; it is hard to tell whether the zero sum of effects is responsible for or is derived from the underlying real-opposition of causes. I hesitate to detect Kant in unwittingly circular reasoning here. (He is, to be sure, the master of intentional circularity in the *Critique*, where the grounds of the possibility of experience are inferred from experience while experience is certified by the grounds. Perhaps the apparent circle in the above paragraph is a precursor of critical thinking.)

The metaphysical intention is, however, quite clear: 1. The world exists as a complex of quantifiably opposed effects; negative magnitudes express such relative opposition; when summed with their positives they yield zero. 2. Underlying these existences, there is a realm of grounds; these are forces, powers and actions; they are also in mutually cancelling opposition, and, like their effects, they are so only relative to each other. 3. In respect to an ultimate ground they are positive, yet no real-opposition to it is possible. Kant himself knows that he has not yet sufficiently clarified the character of *real-grounds*, nor their relation to the divine will.

His first definition of a real-ground actually occurs in a *General Remark* appended to the third, final section of the essay. A logical ground is one whose consequence can be clearly seen through the law of identity; for example, composition is a ground of divisibility, i.e., it is identical with part of the meaning of the concept and can be educed from it analytically. A real-ground, by contrast, has a relation to its effect which, although quite truly expressed as a concept, yet allows no judgment, no true understanding, of the real-ground's mode of action. In other words, the relation of a real cause to its effect is not apprehensible by mere logical analysis. (Here is formulated the problem that Kant will solve in the *Critique* by means of the "synthetic judgment *a priori*"—the cognition in which real connections are made—not, of course, by the logical law of identity but through our cognitive constitution.)

In this essay, this understanding of a real-ground raises— for the first time for Kant—the fundamental question of causation: "How should I understand it THAT, BECAUSE THERE IS SOMETHING, THERE IS SOMETHING ELSE?" The will of God is something. The existing world is something else altogether. Yet the will of God is the ultimate real-ground of the world's existence. Kant says that no talk of cause, effect, power and act will help: God and world are totally each other's other, and yet through one of them the other is posited. And the same holds on a lower level for the natural causes in the world, be they of an event or its cancellation. Kant promises an explication in the future, but for now he remarks only that the relation of real-ground to what is posited or canceled through it cannot be expressed in a judgment, i.e., a mental "representation of the unity of a consciousness of different representations," but is in fact only a mere, non-analyzable concept, that is, a general representation or a thought (*Logic* ¶ 1, 17). Kant is saying that the relation of an effect to its cause cannot be articulated as an affirmed attribution of a predicate to a subject. It is his way of expressing Hume's rejection of empirically grounded causation. (In the *Critique* the attempt to make God's causal relation to the world comprehensible to reason will be shown to be hopeless, but causality within the world will be grounded in the very constitution of the spatial intuition.)

So ends the essay in which the reflection on negative magnitudes has led, through the concept of real-opposition, directly to the problem of causal connection and indirectly to God as ultimate cause. I have not done justice to the exploratory tone of the essay, to Kant's witty derision of those who get stuck in premature dogmatism, and to his sense of having made a mere, even insufficiently explicated, beginning, but a beginning of something very important: the inquiry into causation.

AN ELUCIDATION OF SOME of the matters left unclear in the essay on negative magnitudes occurs in the essay on "The Only Possible Grounds of Proof for a Demonstration of God's Existence" of the same year (1763), and it seems to me so daring that I cannot resist carrying this exposition a little further.

The reflections I shall refer to are not those that most interested Heidegger, the ones concerning existence as position, but those dwelling on the relation of possibility to actuality (or as Kant says, to existence) and on an absolutely necessary "existent" (*Dasein*; First Part, Second and Third Reflections).

Possibility, Kant says, depends entirely on the law of contradiction: That is a possible something the thought of which accords with what is thought in it. This "comparison" of a subject with its predicates through the law of contradiction is to be called *logical* or formal possibility; a triangle cannot have other than three angles, for that would contradict its definition. But it also has something additional, a given character as a triangle in general or in particular, say a right-angled triangle; these are the *data* of its *material* or *real* possibility.

Therewith possibility without prior existence is abolished. For a thing is not only impossible—a "no-thing"—when contradictory predications are made of it, when it is formally impossible, but also when it offers no real material, no *data*, to thinking. For then all thinking ceases, for everything possible must be something thinkable, must offer stuff for thought. It follows that for Kant possibility is conditioned on actuality.

There is, to be sure, no formal inner contradiction in the brute negation of all existence, since nothing has been posited to begin with. But that there be a possibility and that nonetheless nothing actual exist—that *is* contradictory. For if nothing exists, nothing material is given to be thought about. Therefore to say that nothing exists is, according to the previous analysis of existence (*Dasein*) as a positing act of thought, to think and say that there is absolutely nothing. And then to add that something is possible is clearly self-contradictory, for no material for thinking at all is given. Thinking involves material givens; without them it contradicts its own character. Thus the cancellation of the material data of possibility also cancels possibility. *It is absolutely impossible that nothing should exist.* I understand Kant to mean that one can—logically—deny all existence, but having denied it one cannot then retrieve its possibility.

The only really elucidating example of a necessary existence is, Kant says, that of the unique Subject (i.e., God), to be touched on below. Meanwhile, if we ask, for example, how existence precedes possibility in respect to "body," we may grant that the concept body contains no logical impossibility, yet to call on its predicates of extension, impenetrability, force, to be the *data* of possibility (either assumed or experienced) in the absence of actually existing, given bodies, is quite unwarranted. Without such data the concept "body" is empty. (We see here the forerunner of the dictum in the first *Critique* that the mere functions of the understanding are empty without the givens of intuition.)

Then Kant explains the concept of an absolutely necessary existence. To say that it is that whose contradictory is in itself impossible is a merely nominal explanation. Since existence is no predicate, its denial can never conflict with other predicates. However to deny the positing of the thing itself is not a denial of predicates but of something else, and hence is not contradictory. Kant is looking not for logical but "real-necessity" (*Realnotwendigkeit*), for what cannot be denied in any "real-explanation" (*Realerklärung*). This is it: "What I am to regard as absolutely nothing and impossible must be that which eradicates all thinking." Now total nonexistence in fact cancels all the material and data of thought, and hence it is impossible.

It follows that there is an absolutely necessary being. For all possibility assumes something actual, whose cancellation would itself cancel all inner possibility, i.e., the real coherence of predicates. That part of existence, on the other hand, which *does not* provide the material for all that is thinkable, but without which there would still be matter for thought—and thus possibility—that part is, although in a real sense possible, yet in the same sense conditionally possible, i.e., contingent; not *all* existence is necessary. (In his *Inaugural Dissertation* of 1770 Kant will say that all worldly substances are in fact contingent since they maintain reciprocal relations, while necessary beings are independent, ¶ 19.)

Kant now goes on to show that the *one* necessary, non-contingent existence is God, a being that is one, simple, unchangeable, eternal, and a spirit. But its philosophically most important attribute is that it is (in scholastic terms) the *ens realissimum*, the most real being, that which contains the highest reality. For it contains all the givens, the *data*, of possibility either as directly determining other existences or as being the real-ground of which they are the consequences. (In the *Critique*, the *ens realissimum* will be relegated to the status of an ideal of reason, a regulative idea that marshals our thoughts of the world.)

Does the attribution to God of the most and the highest reality mean that *all* realities, i.e., all real attributes, must be assigned to God? Here the concepts of the essay on negative magnitudes come into their own: It is common doctrine that one reality can never contradict another reality, since both are truly affirmed. But this assertion leaves out of account the notion of real-repugnance, i.e., of real-opposition. Realities may, indeed must, oppose each other without one of them being in itself negative.—That was the essay's main finding. In God, however, even real-opposition cannot take place, because that would result in privation or defect and would contradict God's maximal reality. Thus God contains no realities in opposition to his positive predicates; for example, the real-oppositions attributable to bodies, such as being subject to contrary forces, cannot without contradiction belong to a being that has intellect and will; hence the *ens realissimum* has clear positive determinations.

It is, it seems to me, implicit in these pre-Critical essays that neither existence (*Dasein*) nor actuality (*Wirklichkeit*) is as yet convertible with subjective perceptibility, though both will indeed be so later, as Heidegger observes. Instead these terms mean objective givenness, thereness, be it sensorily received or essentially apprehended. The road to the first *Critique* will be the development of this conversion from the object of experience as given *to* the subject to its being constituted *in* the subject. The roots, however, of the primacy of the subject are already present in one respect, now to be shown.

THERE IS, THEN, NECESSARILY a God, a being comprehending not all, but all the highest positive reality. He is a real-ground of the world; the world, in turn, amounts quantitatively to a self-canceled nothing, though it may well be qualitatively positive. One way to get hold of this—by Kant's own frequent confession—still inchoate complex is to ask just how daring a departure from tradition it is.

Kant, who without naming Anselm is attempting to rebut his argument for the existence of God, calls his own proof "ontological" (later in the *Critique* that is what he will call Anselm-type proofs). Anselm argues (*Proslogium* 2, 4) that God is a maximal being whose essence is to be thought as largely and inclusively as possible; thus it must include the predicate existence. This is what Kant denies, but he accepts something that seems to me even deeper in, or rather behind, Anselm's argument: that when *I must think* that God exists, he exists. But this is thinking of the type Kant himself engages in on an even deeper level when he makes God's existence follow from the existential necessities of thinking: What is required for thinking to be possible must necessarily exist. Here Anselm and Kant are brothers under the skin. I can think of counterarguments to their assumption (though without being quite persuaded by them): Is it utterly impossible that a being which *must* exist in thought fails to exist in fact—is it so totally unthinkable? Is it not possible to think that thinking can do utterly without the material, the data grounded either in a highest reality, as in the essay on God's existence, or in some sensory influx from a transcendent outside, as in the first *Critique*? Is it unthinkable that possibilities do not disappear when actualities fail, but that there is spontaneous, autonomous, self-generated, worldless thinking? Kant has, it seems, levered the Cartesian-type certification for personal existence; *Cogito, ergo sum*, "I think, therefore I am," into a proof of God's existence: *Cogito, ergo Deus est*, "I think, therefore there is a God." But what if "I think" entails instead: "*I* make the world," if I myself give myself the *data*?

Such misgivings and intimations aside (they will become Kant's own in the *Opus Postumum*), he has found an approach to a question that seems never to have occupied the ancients and was, as was mentioned, first formulated by Leibniz (*Principles of Nature and Grace*, 7): "Why does something exist rather than nothing? For 'nothing' is simpler and easier than 'something.'" Leibniz finds the answer in the ultimate sufficient reason called God. Kant argues the other way around: Nothing is *harder* than something, indeed impossible for thought, and God becomes necessary not as a sufficient reason inferred from the world's existence but as a necessary being implied by human thinking.

In 1763, having proved in one essay the necessary existence of the highest and most real ground and so (for the time being) answered Leibniz's question, Kant is left with the unanswered next question of the essay on negative magnitudes quoted above, which he prints in block letters: "How can I understand THAT BECAUSE SOMETHING IS, SOMETHING ELSE MIGHT BE?" In other words, having proved God's existence, how can I understand him, or his agents in the world, as causal *grounds*? (This very same question will be presented, as was said, in the *Critique* as unanswerable by logical thinking alone, but solved with the aid of the *a priori* relations given in the intuition.)

By 1781, the year of the first edition of the first *Critique*, Kant will have given up not only his own so circumstantially prepared ontological proof, the only possible one, as he had thought, but also in principle any expectation of a theoretical demonstration of God's existence—and so, it seems, any rational explanation of the first question, why there is existence at all.

The second question, on the other hand, is just what the *Critique* addresses. Kant distinguishes cosmological freedom, the power to make an absolute beginning, from causality according to natural law, which is rule-governed consequence acting within what already exists. An insight into the first, into absolute causation, i.e., creation, Kant shows, is in principle impossible for us, for it is beyond the limits of human reason. The second causality, that of lawful succession, of cause and effect in natural events, is grounded in the synthesizing character of our cognitive constitution. The essays here considered show Kant—and for my part I find this intellectually moving—casting about for disparate clues to the concepts and claims which would one day come to cohere in his master edifice.

6

KANT'S AFTERLIFE

Immanuel Kant, *Opus Postumum*, ed. with an introduction and notes by Eckart Förster, trans. by Eckart Förster and Michael Rosen, in *The Cambridge Edition of the Works of Immanuel Kant* (Cambridge Univ. Press, 1993).
Eckart Förster, *Kant's Final Synthesis: An Essay on the* Opus Postumum (Harvard Univ. Press, 2000).

" BETTER LATE THAN NEVER" is the motto of this review. The work known as the *Opus Postumum* occupied Kant during the last fifteen years of his working life, from 1786 to 1801. (He died at eighty in 1804.) The first English translation, which underlies this review, was published in 1993. The first German printing began in bowdlerized form in a Prussian provincial journal in 1882.

Author's note: This review was written for the alumni of my college, who have *all* read large parts of Kant's writings, and was first published in *The St. John's Review*, vol. XLVII, no. 3 (2004).

1882—that is the year after Michelson and Morley carried out their epoch-making experiment in search of the ether wind that must sweep over the earth if it indeed travels through space filled with some sort of observable matter. It had a dramatic null result. The ether, however, had a huge role in Kant's final project—final in both senses: last and eschatological. Whether Kant's ether is in principle amenable to experiment or not is, to be sure, problematic; nonetheless there is, to my mind, a certain pathos to the posthumous work's first publishing date, a pathos over and above the fact that it took nearly a century to appear.

Eckart Förster's English edition of 1993 (which I should have studied ten years ago) is both an ordering and a selection. Kant left a manuscript, its pages covered in small tight writing with even tinier marginalia, of 527 sheets (1161 pages in the great Prussian Academy edition). The unnumbered leaves had at one time evidently been dropped on the floor. It was a labor to arrange and date them, a task mainly performed by Ernst Adickes in 1916, and then to make the work accessible by judicious selection, which is what Förster has done in the Cambridge edition. The latter effort was called for by the character of Kant's writing—and, evidently, thinking—which is obsessively repetitive, ever circling about the issues in the terminological German of the Critiques glossed by formulaic Latin, only to explode suddenly into astounding new resolutions.

But then, this whole post-Critical legacy is astonishing. In 1790, Kant declared in his third Critique, the *Critique of Judgment*, that here "I conclude my entire Critical enterprise" (¶ 170). Only the dependent metaphysical doctrine was to be worked out, that is, the system of *a priori* cognitions that are implied in the Critical foundations. But almost simultaneously finished business turned into unfinished business.

People who first saw the discombobulated manuscript put about the rumor of Kant's senility. On the contrary: If in the three Critiques we see everything fall into its systematic "architectonic" place, in the *Opus Postumum* we see the foundations of the edifice broken open in the attempt to make the system more encompassing. Not that Kant is countermanding any major postulate of the Critical system but rather that, in the effort to specify it, to make embodied nature and man fall out from it, he opens up its abysses, not only for the enthralled reader but, palpably, for himself—though the one chasm he steps over without the slightest regard is, to my mind at least, the most abysmal one; more of that below. In any case, during the last years, before he stopped writing, Kant seems to have returned not to a second childhood but to a second vigor, to the searching modes of his pre-Critical years.

Here I want to insert a personal note. Whyever, I ask myself, did it take me so long to come to this remarkable work, especially when I was trying to think about Kantian topics: imagination, time, memory, and nonbeing? Well, I sought help in the Critiques and then elsewhere, in Aristotle, Plotinus, Augustine, Russell, Meinong, Husserl. Of the *Opus Postumum* only one—unforgettable—fragment had penetrated to me: "I, the Proprietor of the World." It should have been intimation enough that the Critiques were—possibly—being transcended.

To me Kant had never been primarily the systematician, whose thinking was a relentlessly unificatory construction and whose expression was an intricate terminological rococo. He was rather the philosopher who, more than the self-avowed tightrope dancer Nietzsche, built his edifice over an abyss. I found this the more absorbing since Kant seemed to me the soul of probity, a philosopher of originality *and* rectitude, the rarest of combinations in a vocation whose business ought to be not novelty but truth, though it has occasionally incited its professors to the self-exaltation of invention and the blue smoke of mystification. Kant is the man who reconceived philosophy as *work* (in the essay "On a Refined Tone Recently Raised in Philosophy," 1796). Yet in that sober mode he works himself late in life into strange new territories. Förster, to be sure, ends his book by saying that it is a futile exercise to speculate on the ultimate—unachieved—destination of this last phase. But to me this speculation, though it may well be beyond the reach of scholarship, has a particular attraction: Do these late second sailings, to be found, for example, in Homer (*Odyssey*), Plato (*Laws*), Shakespeare (e.g., *Cymbeline*), Jane Austen (the unfinished *Sanditon*), as well as in Bach and other great musicians, express a necessary development implicit in the work of their *floruits* or novel, adventurous departures into *terra incognita*?

So as not to mystify the reader let me say here, for later amplification, what seems to me the drift of the *Opus Postumum*: It is a drift toward solipsism, the radical self-authorship or "autogenesis" of the human subject and the nature with which it surrounds itself.

Now to Kant's work itself. My advice is to reverse good St. John's practice and to read Förster's explication of the *Opus Postumum* first. It is a conscientious and in places brilliant introduction to what is, after all, an unwieldy, unrevised, and unfinished masterpiece.

Since, however, the *Opus Postumum* takes off from the three Critiques, particularly from the first, the *Critique of Pure Reason* (A edition 1781, B edition 1786), I will give a very stripped-down and tailored version for those few alumni who don't perfectly recall that high point of their junior year (1). Then, since I can make the attraction of the *Opus Postumum* most plausible by listing the above-mentioned rifts and chasms in the first Critique, I will articulate the global perplexities that have always accompanied any local understanding I thought I had achieved (2). Then, with Förster's help, I shall give a brief sketch of the main topics of the *Opus Postumum* (3), which I shall follow with a summary of the way in which Kant's last work confirms or reshapes or resolves my perplexities (4). Finally I will attempt to say a word about the work's bearing on Kant's afterlife in our contemporary thinking (5).

1. Though Kant did not expect, while working on the first Critique (which deals with theoretical reason as it constitutes nature), to write a second Critique on practical reason (that is,

on moral action), it is arguable that his central concern is all along with morality, with human reason as it causes deeds. From that point of view, the mission of the first Critique is to ground a system of deterministic nature in deliberate juxtaposition to the spontaneity of the freedom evinced by the rational will when it acts as it ought, from duty. The realm of nature is a system of necessary and universal rules which we ourselves both constitute and cognize: We can know nature with certainty because we are its authors. (The terms pertaining to this cognition itself rather than to its objects are called "transcendental," or almost synonymously, "Critical": concerned with the conditions that make knowledge possible.) Though the first Critique, as it finally appeared, has as its positive consequence the grounding of experience, meaning the real knowledge of nature, its negative impact is to clear a region for human freedom conceived as autonomy, self-subjection to self-given law. Kant does this by showing that the theoretical understanding and the reason which organizes it are strictly limited to human experience and incapable of dealing with transcendent questions except in terms of "ideals" expressing the human need for completeness.

The crucial difficulty in establishing a sure and certain knowledge of nature is for Kant the doubt cast by Hume on causality: Cause is nowhere to be observed; we see constant conjunctions of events but never necessary interconnections among them. Kant's answer, the crux of his solution, is that we know our way through nature with complete certainty because and insofar as we make it. Thus its laws are ours from "the very first"—*a priori*.

Our cognitive constitution is twofold: by our understanding we think spontaneously (that is, originatingly, out of ourselves) and also discursively (that is, by connecting concepts), thereby unifying manifolds; by our sensibility we are affected receptively by intuitions which are already given as unities. The understanding is thus a formal, logical faculty whose categories are adapted from a well-established tradition. But these categories are empty grasps in the absence of the pure material of the intuition to fill them, where "pure" means unaffected by ordinary sensory influence.

To me this pure, pre-experiential sensibility and its pure, non-sensory matter is Kant's most original, not to say mind-boggling, discovery (or invention—I am as perplexed about it now as ever), for a sensibility is, after all, usually understood to be a capacity for being affected by the senses. It has two branches. The pure "inner" intuition is our sense of time. It is pure because it is analytically prior to sensation. It is "inner" because it is, in ways that become progressively more unclear in the second edition of the Critique and in the *Opus Postumum*, closer to our ego, called the "transcendental apperception," meaning the subject, the I that underlies every object we present to ourselves. For that is what human consciousness means for Kant: presenting objects to ourselves. Self-consciousness or apperception is awareness of the I that is putting this object before itself. It is that awareness which is said in the first Critique to represent itself to us as a phenomenon in inner sense; we know ourselves as phenomenal egos when we attend to numerable time as it ticks away.

The corresponding outer sense is pure space. All we intuit (except ourselves—*so far*) we give the form of space; space is not formal (as is thinking) but *formative*. In this pre-sensory sensorium we find externality within us. Or better, to assume the form of externality objects must be within our receptive sensibility, together with the sensations that give them their quality, the material manifold that gives them body. Nothing could be more contrary to our ordinary sense of things, where "outside" means precisely not within.

What is the purpose of this dizzying reversal, Kant's sequel to the Copernican revolution? That first revolution made the sun stand still and our earth move, while this one makes us again home base, though now the world moves to our measure rather than to a divine maker's plan. Kant's purpose is to bring causality from an outside world, where it is objectively non-observable, into us, where it is subjectively an inherent necessity of our cognitive constitution.

There is a missing step in this sketch, the notoriously fugitive "Schematism of the Pure Concept of the Understanding" (B 176 ff.). It is the crux of the crux of the positive Critique, and its brevity should warn us that something is the matter. Schematizing is the work of the imagination; it is not the capacity for fantasy but a "transcendental" faculty, one that makes knowledge possible. It is, in its depths, responsible for the mystery of conjoining the unconjoinable. It effects this by bringing forth a general diagram (Kant calls it a "monogram") intended to draw together the absolutely disparate effects of the formally functioning understanding and the formatively receptive intuition. Thus time and space are to be conceptualized or, if you like, the concepts of the understanding are to be time- and space-affected.

Kant hurriedly carries out this "dry and boring dissection" for the case of time. For example, *the concept of cause, when time-imbued, becomes the necessary succession of one thing upon another according to a ruling concept.* At this moment the possibility of a causal science that has certainty is grounded. (Here "possibility" does not refer to what *might* happen but to that which enables knowledge to become real.)

Kant silently and completely omits the schematizing of space. I had always supposed that, whatever difficulties I might have, Kant thought it was too easy. I couldn't have been more wrong. Förster shows that it was too hard, and thereby hangs the tale of the *Opus Postumum* (59).

2. First to me among those deep perplexities that give the Critiques their philosophical poignancy have been the space puzzles already alluded to (the underprivileging of space in the Schematism), along with other, related ones.

In the second edition of the first Critique Kant inserted a sort of time bomb, the famous section called the "Refutation of Idealism" (B 274, xxxix), in which he aimed to show that time itself can only be perceived as a determined phenomenon by us when observed against "something permanent in space," that is, against matter: "The consciousness of my own existence is at the same time a consciousness of other things outside me" (B 276). Where, I ask myself, has the first function of the "inner" sense gone? What is now particularly internal about my self-perception?

But so is the very meaning of space as "outer sense" a puzzle. Outerness seems to mean three things at once: It means *extension*, the way a spatial dimension consists of parts outside of each other, stretching away from themselves. It means, second, *externality*, the way objects are experienced as outside of the subject. And it means, third, *outside* and "going beyond" us—the literal sense of "transcendent" (as distinct from "transcendental"), though this is a region in principle unreachable. For what we know, we know *in* us. That is, after all, what Kant intends to show in the negative part of the Critique, the "Transcendental Dialectic," which exposes the illusions reason falls into in going beyond the limits of our experience—and is thus the *critique* of pure reason proper.

There is, second, a puzzle that arises incidentally from the multivalence of Critical terms. The categories, Kant repeats emphatically, have no being on their own and achieve meaning only as they grasp intuitive material. Take then the category of unity which imposes oneness on manifolds of sense. There is, however, also the unity that reason strives for as an ideal but can reach only illusorily. And there is "the synthetic unity of apperception," the unifying work of the subject deep beneath appearance, its chief theoretical effect. Whence, we might ask, does Kant get the notion of unity to begin with? Is there not something suspect about this transcendental notion—and others, for example, "thing"—which are necessary to establish the transcendental terms of the Critiques but which are in traditional metaphysics terms of transcendence, the attributes of Being that are beyond sensory experience? How does Kant come to know these terms of Critical thought that are antecedent to properly certified knowledge?

A third enigma is immediately connected with the space puzzles. The dialectic of reason is intended to clear the decks for human freedom and for the exercise of practical reason, which expresses itself in deeds. But the system of nature grounded in the positive part of the Critique is deterministic. There are no loose joints. How then does moral action *appear* in the natural world? How does it actually change events determined by natural laws? How do we as moral beings insert ourselves into, intervene in, nature? Further, where, in fact, are we in the world as phenomenal, perceiving subjects? In the *Critique of Pure Reason* there is matter, but no bodies, human or natural—nor in the second Critique, that of Practical Reason. The simultaneous actuality of moral deed and natural events is a mystery: How does the practical reason make our muscles do the right thing?

The fourth open question is this: How far is nature specified by the Critical grounds and their ensuing principles? Are the types of forces necessarily operating in nature specifiable, and are their mathematical laws determinable *a priori*? How thoroughgoing are the grounds of possibility, or in Kant's terms: Can a complete metaphysical doctrine of nature be worked out such as will descend to and determine the actual laws of physics? But then, what of observation, what of contingency? Is anything not under our own rules? Is the world *nothing* but our mirror?

Thence arises the fifth question, truly a mystery. Whence comes the matter of sensation which fills our space with its quantities and qualities and reflects to us our time by being the permanent material background against which motions appear? Is the occasion for the appearance of this matter infused into us transcendently, from beyond, or are we its authors not only formally, formatively, but really, substantively? I would say that this is the most unregarded, the *totally* unregarded, question in Kant's writing—and in his thought as well: Are we, after all, buffeted by transcendent influxes? Or are we, when all has been worked out, shown to be our own authors in every respect—which would be brute solipsism, the philosophy of *solus ipse* "I alone, by myself"? But then what becomes of the ideal republic of mutually respectful moral beings and of the real political community of embodied human beings? What access do we then have to each other's subjectivity?

Finally, the sixth problem, not of doctrine but of argumentation: In the first Critique God is an ideal of reason, a required hypothesis or postulate if we are to act morally, an "as if" representation whose existence is to us a necessary thought though its actuality is provably unprovable. As Kant works on the *Opus Postumum* the thought of a necessary God is increasingly sharpened and the claim more pointed, as shown in III: There are reasons that drive us to think that God is necessary; thus God's existence must be first postulated and then acknowledged as real. He is actual for us: *Est Deus in nobis*, "There *is* a God—*in us*" (my dash and italics, *O.P.* 209, 248). And: "Everything that thinks has a God." That is to say, thinking requires a divinity and what thinking requires it must have—but only for the thinker. I simply cannot make out whether this God *really* exists or is after all what Kant himself would call a "subreption," a surreptitious rustling of Being by a needy reason, or perhaps some third being I am too literal-minded to comprehend. To me it is marvelous how scintillatingly ambiguous the severely systematic Kant really is at great junctures.

Whether the above items are enigmas, questions, problems, puzzles, they each open up abysmal depth for the inquiry concerning human knowledge, action, and faith. Except for the spectacularly absent fifth question, concerning the origin of sensation and its stimulating matter, the *Opus Postumum* will show Kant grappling with these problems, sometimes only to focus them the more pressingly.

3. The early title of the *Opus Postumum* was "Transition from the Metaphysical Foundations of Natural Science to Physics." The final title is "The Highest Standpoint of Transcendental Philosophy in the System of Ideas: God, the World, and Man in

the World, Restricting Himself through Laws of Duty" (Förster xliii). The distance between the titles betokens Kant's winding himself from system-driven, downward doctrinal specification into ascending, comprehensive speculation. An obvious question will be whether these speculations in the main confirm or undermine the Critical enterprise. I want to say here that either way it is a thrilling business. If the gaping holes in the architecture of the system can be stopped and the foundations reinforced, the edifice will surely be the more magnificent and rivaled only by Hegel's system. (I omit Aristotle, not so much because his philosophizing historically preceded the notion of philosophic system-making, but because he would in any case have thought that first philosophy should be problem- rather than system-driven.) But if Kant is impelled to let his own system implode the outcome surely glows with the sober glory of thought outthinking itself. In the event, it seems to be a little of both.

The first question that has occupied students of the *Opus Postumum* concerns the project of the title. Why was a transition needed, where was there a gap? The *Metaphysical Foundations of Natural Science* of 1786 seemed to provide a doctrinal transition from the general principles of the first Critique (which ground the laws of action and reaction, of causation in time and of the conservation of matter, "Analogies of Experience," B 218 ff.) to the specific Newtonian Laws of Motion. That is to say, Kant has "constructed" these proto-laws, which means he has exhibited them in the intuition so as to display their necessary characteristics. Why, then, does this transition require another Transition?

Förster gives a thoroughly satisfying answer (59 ff.). As we saw, the spatial schematization of the categories is missing in the first Critique. The *Metaphysical Foundations* is in fact this missing schematism, the spatialization of the categories; I omit the details of Förster's proof, but the argument is on the face of it convincing. At this point matter comes in: Kant must analyze empirical matter and its motion and then "construct" or "exhibit" the concept so obtained in space. (This is an epicy-cle in the so-called Critical circle: Kant analyzes the object, here matter, he intends to certify cognitively and then provides its transcendental conditions of possibility.)

But in order for matter not just to occupy and traverse space but to act dynamically (as it is empirically observed to do), to compact itself into bodies capable of moving each other, the forces of matter must be established. But forces are not to be observed as appearances (as Hume insisted) and are thus not constructible, that is, exhibitable as configurations in the intu-ition. The *Metaphysical Foundations* do not succeed in solving the problem of cohesive bodies (as opposed to shapeless mat-ter) held dynamically within their boundaries and exercising attractive as well as repulsive force on each other. Thus this metaphysical transition cannot present physics with its basic concepts. A gap bars the way to the categories' objective valid-ity, that is, to their empirical applicability; the attempted sche-matism is incomplete.

So a large part of the early work on the *Opus Postumum* is devoted to the Tantalus-labor of finding, *a priori*, the kinds and ratios of forces that will underwrite our natural world of dynamically moving cohesive bodies. Clearly Kant now intends (or always did) for the Critical grounding to reach very far into empirical, supposedly adventitious (unpredictable) cognition. We may wonder what will survive that passage between the Scylla of complete systematicity and the Charybdis of empiri-cal science.

Now come the ether proofs, a huge and weighty presence in the *Opus Postumum*. From a certain point on, Kant regards it as established that ether (or caloric), an "imponderable, inco-hesible, inexhaustible," medium that is *"universally distributed, all-penetrating,* and *all-moving"* (O.P. 98, 92) is the condition of possibility of all the mechanical forces of matter whose effects (if not they themselves) are apparent in the making and the motions of bodies. Förster has lucidly reconstructed the intricate essential proof from its many sites and disparate approaches in the text (89 ff.). It is worth attending to in spite of the negative Michelson-Morley ether experiment of 1881, not merely because it makes vivid the exigencies of the transcendental system (a system which someone—not myself—might indeed regard as having merely historical interest), but because it is the result of a deep meditation on the conditions of spatial experience.

To begin with, Förster points out that the *Opus Postumum* reverses the first Critique on the source of the unity of all appearances (84). In that Critique it was an ideal of reason to bring unity into our necessarily piecemeal perception. Then, in the third Critique, the *Critique of Judgment* (1719), a new source of unity comes on the scene: Nature herself is purposive and systematic. Under the influence of this reversal from reason ideally unifying nature to nature herself really unifying its forces into a system, a strange new situation arises. (The ultimate possibility of its arising I would trace back, without having worked it out sufficiently, to the above-mentioned ambivalence of the term "unity" in the first Critique: Is unity a subjective function or a transcendent characteristic of beings?) This situation is that nature herself must now contain *a priori* principles of its objective possibility; no longer are all *a priori* conditions of experience in the subject.

Or are they? Förster is inclined to think that the ether, as a condition of possibility of a system of nature (and hence of its science, physics) is an ideal of our reason, hence subjective (91–92). But he does not deny that Kant himself wavered and sometimes speaks of the underlying medium as existing "outside the idea" (*O.P.* 82); this oscillating effect is not unlike that of Kant's treatment of God's existence (see below).

The chief elements of the existence proof for the ether are as follows. From the subjective side: Empty space is not perceptible; a single space filled with moving forces is the condition of the possibility of unified experience which is knowledge of connected perceptions; hence we must form the idea of an elementary material that is in space and time and has the characteristics listed above; thus we get a subjective principle of the synthetic unity of possible experience such as must under-lie physics.

From the objective side: Nature is the complex of all things that can be the objects of our senses and hence of experience, and we do have experience of outer objects. But experience requires that its objects form, for our judgments, a system which has a necessary unity according to one principle. The ether, distributed through space yet forming a collective whole, is the one and only candidate for such a system. Therefore, as making the whole of experience possible, it is actual.

Thus the ether is a unique—and *very* peculiar—external object that really exists in the—to my mind—oscillating way of Kant's existence proofs, which argue from the enabling grounds of knowledge to the real existence of the object. As a ground of possibility it is not itself perceptible or observable. Thus Kant might have replied to Michelson-Morley that, since the ether hypothesis was the condition of all experiments, it was itself not falsifiable by experiment. But they, as presumably positivist physicists, would have turned this reply around and said that what is not falsifiable is not positive knowledge. To me, too, the transcendental ether is, as I said, illuminating less as a real ground of science than as a reflection on the nature of our experience of space and its contents. For isn't it the case, after all, that the material ether having been eradicated from physics, other fillers of space had to be found, such as fields of force and geometric conformations of space itself?

In any case, Kant considers that the specific dynamic properties he assigns to his ether solve the problem of systematizing the mechanical forces, attraction, repulsion, cohesion, whose effects are mathematicized in the Newtonian manner. The—surely superseded—details of this grounding are obscure to me and I can summon interest in the argument about them only insofar as they realize that "transition," announced in the early title of the *Opus Postumum*, from the metaphysical doctrine of perceptible matter in motion to bodies subject to an *a priori* determinable system of forces.

And now Kant realizes that a question looms that will have made a reader of the *Critique of Pure Reason* and of the ensuing *Metaphysical Foundations of Natural Science* uneasy all along: However does a scientist get wind of this now systematically embodied nature? How does the subject come to *know* its now exhaustively knowable external object?

This realization brings on a pivotal moment in the later fascicles of the *Opus Postumum*, when the *Selbstsetzungslehre*, the "doctrine of self-positing," comes to the fore. Again, Förster is a much-needed guide through the text (101–16).

The terms of the first Critique are, all in all, well marshalled—systematic and precise—within the work; it is when we think beyond it that they become scintillatingly obscure. We might worry that we are undercutting Kant's explicit intention in thus thinking outside the box. The later *Opus Postumum* shows us Kant doing it himself. One might go so far as to say that the older he got the more radically he thought (which, rightly considered, is the way it ought to be).

The late work reconsiders self-consciousness, at first in the spirit of the Critique, but then in increasingly more boldly enunciated ways. Everything begins with "I think," the self-recognition of the subject. It is a piece of mere logical analysis (since no intuition is involved) by which I make myself into an object to myself (*O.P.* 182). So stated this first transcendental event makes me ask myself: Can so momentous a self-diremption, that of exercising my autonomy in making myself into my own object, occur by a *merely* logical act, the analysis of the meaning of "I think"? Doesn't it require some onto-logical activity? Kant answers this question, though along Critical rather than metaphysical lines. The first act can occur only *together* with a second one: This is an act of synthesis, meaning one in which thought grasps and unifies something given that goes beyond mere logic—to begin with, pure time and space. In space and time the subject posits itself, or better the subject posits itself as an "I." This is the doctrine of self-positing.

To appreciate how astounding this doctrine is we must look

at the notion of positing. For Kant, to posit is to *assign* existence, the one and only way to *realize* existence (an identification that goes way back to an essay on the proofs of God's existence of 1763, see the previous essay). Thus in self-positing I bring myself into existence. It is an act of self-creation. This way of putting it tells me that existence is a subordinate condition depending on a somehow prior subject which is, however, itself not—or is not knowable as—a being that has an essence, an actuality, or, so far, personhood. The I-subject is a mystery into which Kant himself proscribes inquiry in his critique of dialectical reason.

So far, however, though I exist, I have not yet made it into the natural world. This is where the ether does its service. It makes space real to the senses, filled as it is with a universal protomatter that is the condition of connected perceptions wherever I find myself in it. Space is thus not only the subjective form of sensation but a real unified object outside me, unified by the ubiquitous presence of a weightless, unbulkable ether.

And yet I, in turn, am in it. For as space becomes perceptible because of the ceaseless dynamism of its system of ether-grounded forces, so I can perceive it, since I myself am an organic body that is sensitive to forces because this body is itself a system of organized forces: To get sensation I must be sensitive, to get sensations from a dynamic system I must be such a system myself—I must be continuous with nature.

Here at last is the embodied subject *in* the world. Self-positing thus has a second phase. As I made myself exist within my pure cognitive constitution, so I posit myself as affected by forces that I have organized to enable me to experience nature: "Positing and perception, spontaneity and receptivity, the objective and subjective relations are simultaneous because they are identical as to time, as appearances of how the subject is *affected*—thus are given *a priori* in the same *actus*" (*O.P.* 132). Förster observes that the last phrase means that the same original transcendental act brings about the duality of empirical self and material world. Because in apprehending the undetermined material manifold I insert into it certain fundamental forces, I can simultaneously represent myself as an affected body and as so affected by an external cause (107).

So it seems that the system finally has closed in on the human body from the inside out through the transcendental spatial intuition and from the outside in through the "hypostatized" forces of nature (meaning forces "supposed, but as real"): the elementary dynamical ether and the mechanical forces of physics known against its ethereal ground. Better late than never, though this body be merely a self-moving machine, which, incidentally, responds to impinging outside forces as would a system of rigid and moving parts. The subject has now called into existence not only itself but also its world and its body—has made itself aware of itself as a certified knower and simultaneously as a participating inhabitant of perceptible space. Perceptibility, however, is just what existence means for Kant: existence is a by-product of the relation between a cognitive subject and the object it posits for itself, even outside itself. I would put the puzzle here thus: How real can such existence be, in the ordinary meaning of the word, that is, indefeasibly and self-assertively independent of me? Yet Kant would find, had found, such a question offensively obtuse, since it voids the whole Critical enterprise and its compelling motives. Nonetheless, it does seem that in setting the limits of reason Kant has abolished the finitude of human autonomy, the finitude that implies something beyond me which I am not.

Förster interprets the doctrine of self-positing as a schema for (perceptible) outer space (114), since a schema brings together the spontaneous understanding with the receiving sensibility, in this case, matter- or sensation-filled space. This schema completes the conditions for a science of nature—though something else is missing.

There is as yet no personhood. But since persons are subjects to which deeds can be imputed, since they are moral, that is, free and responsible beings, and since one purpose of the whole enterprise was to ground human freedom and with it morality, Kant is driven to a second, a moral self-positing and, hard upon it, yet beyond, to a focusing of the idea of God. More precisely, from the start of this final part of Kant's last work these two topics, human morality and God, are more intimately related than they ever were in the *Critique of Practical Reason*. For there God is merely a postulate of practical reason (2.2.5), a kind of by-thought, required because nature by herself offers no ground for assuring us of happiness commensurate with our deserts. So we must believe that there is a cause, working outside of nature, that will bring about such a reward. But the moral necessity of God is subjective, that is, it is a need, not an objective ground of duty or belief. In the *Opus Postumum* it is as if man, having brought himself, his world, and himself-in-the-world into existence, was now ready to posit God as well.

But there are more serious, systematic reasons for Kant to turn to God in his last work. The said postulate of the second Critique calls upon God as a condition of making moral actions achievable for humans. Förster traces the various functions God is assigned (summarized on pp. 134–35). The last of these, stemming from Kant's *Religion within the Boundaries of Mere Reason* (1793), is that of God as founder of an ethical commonwealth. But in the *Opus Postumum* Kant says repeatedly that the divine power cannot make a man morally good: "He must do it himself" (*O.P.* 249). So here opens what Kant himself calls an "abyss of a mystery"; Förster interprets this phrase as Kant's realization that human moral autonomy and God as founding father of an ethical commonwealth are in contradiction (133). Kant finds a way out, adumbrated in *Religion* and sharpened in the late *Opus Postumum*.

The self-positing so far described had been theoretical, cognitive. But now Kant introduces a second, moral-practical self-positing, analogous to the first in having its own *a priori* moving forces: the ideas of right that unite all persons, as expressed in the Categorical Imperative (which commands, unconditionally, the subjection of individual inclination to laws acknowledged as universal, *O.P.* 198); the difference is only that the first involves being affected by outer, spatial forces, the second consists of obedience to one's own rationality—self-forcing, one might say. Self-positing, recall, was bringing oneself into existence by becoming conscious at once of oneself as thinking and as being affected by objects determined by oneself. So too moral self-positing is self-consciousness together with the consciousness that I can subjugate my inclinations and can myself determine my will, that is, choose morally—which is what Kant calls freedom.

Kant now argues that the idea of human freedom, whose force is formulated in the Categorical Imperative, brings with it immediately, analytically, the concept of God. For the imperative is a command, which, like the law of a civil commonwealth, unites all rational beings, and therefore it requires a law-giver and enforcer. Thus God must exist, and to do as we ought (that is, our duty) is a divine command.

But God's existence is not that of a being independent of human reason (Förster 142). Rather, just as we postulated an ether to make a system of forces possible, so we postulate God as real to give the idea of duty a moving force. Thus the contradiction of human freedom and divine imposition certainly seems to be resolved.

There is one more step to be taken. God is now an ideal of practical reason, said, however, to exist—in some way. What is the divinity's relation to nature, particularly human nature? This is Kant's "abyss of a mystery," mentioned above: God and the world are heterogeneous ideas; as God cannot make men better, for that would abrogate their moral freedom, so he cannot interfere with nature, for that would abrogate its lawful determinateness. Kant reaches for the solution we would now expect: The unification of God and nature lies in the human subject. It is to be found in "Man in the World, Restricting Himself Through Laws of Duty," as the penultimate title page puts it (O.P. 244). He is an ideal, an archetype; the wise man, the philosopher, who knows God in himself *and* the laws of nature *and* the imperative of action. Kant has been, significantly it now turns out, in the habit of using the term *Welt-weisheit*, "world-wisdom," for philosophy. With the human ideal Kant has reached "The Highest Standpoint of Transcendental Philosophy." Förster says he has therewith solved one of the oldest problems of philosophy, how to unify theoretical and practical reason (146). And so he has—if we can comprehend this solution.

From *Religion* on through the *Opus Postumum* Kant has been emphasizing the importance of a human ethical community superintended by God to the realization of morality. In the latter work, it is this union of rational beings that makes the force of moral law analogous to the unifying ether of the natural system. Since now man has finally turned up in the body, a major enigma of the *Critique of Practical Reason* appears to be resolved: How transcendental subjects, each, moreover, locked within its own self-constituted natural world, can ever appear and speak to each other.

I say the enigma *appears* to be solved because the subject is now embodied and has material appearance. But that doesn't really help: How does my appearing body enter your self-posited world—unless we hypostasize, very seriously, a true outside, a transcendent Beyond, through which I can come to you by infusing your intuition with a sensory manifold expressing my person in an appearance? But this is language so alien to Kant that I am almost abashed to use it. Nonetheless, the grounds of that intersubjective communication without which Kant cannot conceive an ethical community—a human one, at least—are missing from the Transcendental System. This enigma is clearly conjoined to that of another's body, because before we apprehend each other as rational beings we must appear to each other as material bodies. For we have no way (short of entering each other's minds) of conveying thought except in embodied form.

Nor is the God implied in our recognition of "human duties as divine commands" intelligible to me. This subjective God induces in me a desire to get down to brass tacks: Is a god who is "the inner vital spirit of man in the world" (*O.P.* 240) a God who exists in any ordinary sense, that is, a God who is a stand-alone substance, who is there, in his realm, whether I exist or not?

Kant refuted, more than once, Anselm's proof that God exists (e.g., in the *Critique of Pure Reason* B 626), because it depends on regarding existence not as the subject's positing of an object but as a property of the object itself; thus Anselm argues that in conceiving God we must necessarily include his existence in his essence. Yet it seems to me that Kant has accepted a precondition of Anselm's proof, namely that when thought necessarily conceives of (and therefore conceives necessarily) the object as existing, then it must exist—only where Anselm would say "beyond me," Kant says "in my thought." Is this an argument that gains anything as it goes? I think the final pages of his life's work, preoccupied though it is with God-positing, show no sign that this question oppressed Kant, that he felt an insufficiency in the thought that the unifier of all realms is the dutiful man who has God within but is otherwise left on his own, is "his own originator" (*O.P.* 209) and also the maker of Heaven and Earth—except that once he says this: "There is a certain sublime melancholy in the feelings which accompany the sublimity of the ideas of pure practical reason" (*O.P.* 212).

4. Here, to conclude, is a summary review of the perplexities that I found in the Critiques and of the bearing the *Opus Postumum* has on them.

First, the space puzzles. The *Opus Postumum* acknowledges what the transcendental Critiques had, *ipso facto*, no place for: that if the transcendental subject is to be affected by sensation through, or better, in its sensibility, it must be embodied. Kant now puts the subject's body in space so that through its own forces it may interact with the forces of nature. This somatic positing quite literally fleshes out the system, and it does so by fixing on one of the several meanings of "external" that "outer sense" seems to carry in the first Critique: As one would expect, Kant now sometimes speaks as if the ether-filled space, where my body meets nature's bodies, were in some real sense *outside of myself* as subject. That cannot be, however, since space never ceases to be what it was in the first Critique, the pure content (so to speak) of our receptive outer sense, the spatial intuition. But that fact results in this strangely involuted condition: The body, through which the world affects me, is *within* this Kantian sensorium, the intuition, the spatial sensibility; so we project a body within ourselves to receive sensations from an "outer" world we have ourselves created (Kant's own term, e.g., *O.P.* 235). I keep asking myself how Kant would have responded to this construal of the post-Critical layout. Would we could raise the dead!

On the second, more general, question concerning the origin and fixing of the transcendental terms that stake out the system, the *Opus Postumum* is silent, though Kant asks himself over and over what transcendental philosophy is—his very last proposed title (at least in Förster's selection) is "Philosophy as a Doctrine of Science in a Complete System." The question I am asking could be put like that: Where does the philosopher stand when he establishes "The Highest Standpoint of Transcendental Philosophy"? If Kant considered this question he does not say—perhaps he would have thought it madness, much as Aristotle thinks it is ridiculous to try to show that there *is* nature (*Physics* 2.1).

The third question, "How is moral action actually inserted into a deterministic natural world?," is in fact answered in the *Opus*: The rational subject exerts a moral force analogous to natural forces. But is it an answer? How exactly does the force of reason move bodies? Psychokinetically?

My fifth question, "Whence comes adventitious sensation and hence that contingency of nature which makes science empirical in detail?," is simply and spectacularly untouched in the *Opus Postumum*, as it was in the Critiques. Yet it is not an unreasonable problem to raise, because, though Kant likes to describe what it is that comes to us as a mere "manifold" (manyness simply), sensation is in fact the material of specific appearances; hence, as it seems to me, *some* sort of evidence for its origin must be forthcoming (for from antiquity on, appearance is appearance *of* something, that is to say, is evidence and screen at once of something beyond it).

One motive for drawing sensation more and more into the subject is precisely the principled specification of natural science: The more detail comes under the subject's control the more transcendentally grounded physics becomes, that is, the more it can anticipate its findings and make laws by analogy. As it is, the ether theory goes pretty far in prescribing, *a priori*, the types of mechanical force whose effects are to be noticed in bodies, even up to dictating some of their mathematical laws, for example the inverse square law of attraction: Kant explains that the following argument holds for any force that is diffused from the center of force through concentric spherical shells. Since the spherical surfaces vary as the square of their radii, the larger the sphere, that is the more distant from the center, the less will be the force distributed over each unit surface. Thus the effect of the force will vary inversely as the square of the distance or as $1/r^2$ (*Met. Found.* ¶ 519).

Could it be that Kant might be driven to say that we ourselves are the creators of our sense material? In the *Prolegomena to Any Future Metaphysics* (1783) he distinguishes *bounds* that are positive in having an enfolding Beyond, from *limits* that are mere negations. In that work he says that metaphysics leads to bounds beyond which lie the "things in themselves," which are inaccessible to experience and cognition because they are beyond our cognitive faculties, but which it is nonetheless necessary to assume as sources, presumably, among other things, of sensation (¶ 57). In the *Opus Postumum* that Beyond seems to have receded; then must we ourselves be the generators of sensation? Might we be driven to suppose that the unknowable transcendent noumenal I is itself the source of the sensations that affect me? And if so, how is Kant's system in that respect different from Fichte's *Science of Knowledge*, in which the subject is completely self-posited, including its sensory affects, and of which Kant says that he regards it "as a totally indefensible system . . . for the attempt to cull a real object out of logic is a vain effort" (*O.P.* 264)? Call it absolute idealism or solipsism, in putting the world in man it leaves him *solus*, a subject alone without a confronting object, and Kant seems to find that insupportable in the Fichtean system. Recall from hints above that the first Critique itself was already vulnerable to the charge of solipsism. Sartre, for example, in the chapter "The Reef of Solipsism" in *Being and Nothingness* (3.1.2), raises it with respect to time, insofar as it is an inner sense: How then can a Kantian "I" be synchronous with any "Other"?

I want to insert a reflection here. Philosophers pride themselves on following wherever honestly consequential thinking leads, even into the insufferable. There came generations after Kant who took a kind of unholy joy in their desperate conclusions. But Kant is the philosopher of "conditions of possibility," of finding the terms that enable the satisfaction of rational humanity. So I imagine him to be open to the question: *Quo vadis?*, "Where are you going?" For that the love of wisdom should turn out to be totally self-love seems indeed to be insufferable.

Finally, the sixth perplexity, the proof, no, rather the positing of the existence of God: In the first Critique the *understanding*, our faculty for organizing given material into experience, sets the starting terms; the theoretical *reason* is considered mainly as a faculty for attempting, indefeasibly, to marshal judgments connecting these terms into inevitably illusory syllogistic conclusions. In the *Opus Postumum*, however, the practical reason is paramount, for its requirements come to be dominant. It leads the way in the positing of self, body, and finally God. This God-positing is no longer the "as-if" postulation of Kant's moral works, which entitles us to act merely as if there were a God who sanctions and rewards. In the *Opus Postumum* reason is compelled to posit God as actual—though in me and not as a substance. Actual though not substantial, subjective but an object—I seem to lack the intellectual wherewithal for entertaining these conjunctions. Indeed, one of the benefits of entering into the ratiocinative preoccupations of a Kant, who explores and pushes his own concepts to their limits and who is moreover—as I think—incapable of mere invention or simple confusion, is that one is confronted in precise and compelling terms with the limits of intelligibility.

5. The Kant we study as a community is and will continue to be the Kant of the two Critiques of Pure and Practical Reason, and so it will be, I think, for most students of philosophical works. Thus Kant's influence on the thinking world (where attention to Kant is growing rather than waning, for example in cognitive science and in ethics) will be mostly Critical.

That Kant had a living post-Critical afterlife is in itself a source of fascination, which the review has tried to express. The *Opus Postumum*, however, though it may never, and probably should not, exert the direct influence of the Critiques, also contributes to Kant's posthumous afterlife, not so much, as I said, in directly *influencing* the thinking of people now alive, as in *projecting* a drift that is being realized among us.

I am referring primarily to the topic of subjectivity. In many departments of life the outcome of a venture is an advance over the beginning—which is called progress. In philosophy, however, the working-out of the origin is often a shallowfication, to coin a term. One reason is precisely that philosophy is treated as progressive, which entails either contracting the deep open questions of original inquiry into more effectively resoluble tight problems, or, on the contrary, loosening the precisely significant terms of a coherent philosophy to connote its bowdlerized, or at least more relaxed, possibilities. Kant's terms are more liable to the latter fate.

For Kant expands, late in life, and late in the *Opus Postumum*, on what he had asserted earlier: "Philosophy is to be regarded either as the *habitus* of philosophizing or as a work: through which there arises, proceeding from it, a work as a system of absolute unity" (247; I can't resist quoting a neighboring entry, which shows Kant in what he would call a "technical-practical" mode, that is, displaying mundane practicality—always an index of mental alertness: "N.B. The melon must be eaten today—with Prof. Gensichen—and, at this opportunity, [discuss] the income from the university.") Consequently Kant's terms are from the beginning well-defined and well-seated in a system, and thus apt to descend to the public by acquiring more diffuse rather than narrower usages.

System-building is out of style at the present moment; the mood is anti-foundationalist. Particularly out of favor in philosophy are the two great Critical assumptions, the one so deep beneath Kant's thinking that there is no overt reflection on it in the Critiques, the other perhaps the central preoccupation of the *Opus Postumum*. The former is representationalism, the apprehension of thinking as the activity of putting objects before the cognitive faculties; the German for "representation" is *Vorstellung*, literally "setting [something] before [oneself]." (I should mention that representationalism at least is alive and well in the cognitive *sciences*, as opposed to philosophy.) The latter assumption is the one expressed in the quotation above, that the work of philosophy is "architectonic," the building of a well-grounded, completely unified, and thoroughly detailed edifice representing the activities and aspects of the rational subject, the "I." (To be sure, Kant's system is only the penultimate great Continental system; in the ultimate one, however, that of Hegel, the dialectic of concepts supersedes representational thinking, and the system is not constructed architectonically but develops organically.)

Three hugely influential shapes that the "I" as an object of reflection has taken are: the Cartesian *Ego*, a thing that knows of its existence as it thinks and can apply itself to mathematicizable spatial extension; the Rousseauian *Self*, a pure interiority that knows and revels in its mere sense of existence; and a Kantian *Subject*, an I that knows itself in two capacities, as theoretical (the subject of formal thinking and of a formative sensibility which together give laws to external nature), and as practical (an autonomous person that gives the law to itself as a moral actor).

All three, Cartesian quantification, Rousseauian self-concern and Kantian personhood, have been absorbed and naturalized into contemporary thinking. The subject of the Critiques, however, being the most complex and comprehensive of these ideas, has also been most liable to second-hand connotations. For example, the word "subjective" evidently got into general philosophical and hence into common use through the Critiques, though when we say something is "purely subjective" we tend to mean it in a denigrating sense: lacking hard, public objectivity.

But the expanded terms of the *Opus Postumum* are not, as far as my reading goes, known to our contemporaries—the work has, after all, been available for barely a decade—neither to the proponents of human self- and world-construction nor to the post-Nietzschean value-relativists who hold some version of the idea that man himself is the creator of values, or the religious thinkers who regard God as a self-granted response to human need. Yet all these notions are in a more disciplined, systematic form adumbrated in the *Opus Postumum:* in the self-positing of the subject and its world-construction, in the autonomy of its moral life, and in the required postulation of its God.

But in what mode, to return to a question asked in the beginning, has Kant thus become the occulted projector of our modernity? Did he succumb—Förster thinks this implausible (76)—to the then-current craze of "posito-mania" (*Setzkrankheit*)? Is he spinning out the deep implications of the Critical enterprise, perhaps into originally unintended consequences and to his own uneasy amazement? Or has he, in adventurous old age, leapt beyond the Critiques into the stormy oceans that he once said surrounded the land of the pure understanding, an island of truth enclosed by the unchangeable bounds of nature (*Critique of Pure Reason*, B 294)?

These questions I am in principle unable to answer for myself, because I am not sure whether there can be a philosophical system with joins so tightly fitted that its inherent necessities are unambiguously fixed, and, in particular, because the transcendental system of the *Opus Postumum* offers surprises (the ether), superadded requirements (the specification of empirical physics), shortfalls of closure (the source of sensation). Nor am I certain in general whether, when a philosopher takes a structure of thought to a new level either by fine-tuning its technicalities or by driving it to its ultimate conclusions, he is doing the work of interpretation or of deconstruction. Instead I want to express this, my sense of Kant's late unfinished work: If "awe" signifies a mixture of admiration and unease, here is the occasion to recall a good word to its proper use, and to say that the *Opus Postumum* is indeed awesome.

7

Depth Versus Complexity

W HAT A GREAT HONOR it is to be invited to speak to the philosophers of Athens, though I came flying into Atlanta through the blue skies by airplane rather than sailing into the Piraeus over the wine-dark sea by trireme!

My topic is a duality, an opposition in the way our world offers itself to the search for knowledge, which is mirrored in our personal predisposition for a way of inquiry.

I've learned not to expect an audience to sit with bated breath until I reveal my own inclination and also not to indulge myself in post-modern indeterminacies. So I'll say up front where, as my students say, I'm "coming from" and, as matters more, where I'm going with my title, "Depth Versus Complexity." I think that the single dimension of depth describes such bottom-seeking knowledge as we're capable of searching out; it may be called *philosophia*, "love of wisdom." The two dimen-

The author delivered this lecture at the Department of Philosophy of the University of Georgia in Athens, Georgia, in September 2016.

Tomb of the Diver, Posidonia (modern Paestum), c. 480–470 B.C.E., Museum, Paestum

sions of complexity, or *spread*, on the other hand, describe such surface-covering *information* as we can attain by research; it could be named, to coin a term, *philotechnosyne*, "love of skillful [fact]-finding."

Since it seems to me hazardous, both aimless and dangerous, to plunge into the depths below a surface that I'm not acquainted with, it also seems to me that those who attempt such a plunge, which is always made with eyes closed, should have their eyes wide open above and be acquainted with much of the wide surface—always keeping in mind Heraclitus' dictum that "eyes and ears are bad witnesses to humans that have barbarian souls" (Fr. D-K 107). I will cite rather, in behalf of being extensively informed, Socrates, who lived in that first Athens as an ardent urbanite. He seems to Phaedrus, his ostensible guide, like a stranger outside the city in the country around Athens, and he *says* that he, Socrates, only learns when within the city; but he *shows* that he has far more real local knowledge than his companion.

The direct opposite of complexity is simplicity; of depth, it is shallowness. I do not disavow but rather prefer to avoid those antitheses for now. So I'll describe the two ways not as directly opposite, but rather as orthogonal to each other (that is, at right angles). Let me begin in a somewhat unlikely way: by envisioning the most basic Cartesian coordinate diagram of classical physics, in which the horizontal x-axis represents the fundamental independent variable, time, and the vertical y-axis, which is orthogonal to it, represents some other physical dimension—early on, distance, velocity, and acceleration. That's so even in today's elementary textbooks. But at a crucial moment in physics, its first modern moment, the direction changes. The second theorem of the Third Day of Galileo's *Two New Sciences* (1638) sets out, under the title "Naturally Accelerated Motion," the earliest clearly quantified law of nature, namely, that for free fall at the surface of the earth, where acceleration is naturally uniform.[1] Here time is represented by an *upright* line, while the horizontal stands for velocity. Moreover, time begins not at what will later be called the *origin*, the intersection of the representative lines, but at a release point. Picture the diagram as rendering Galileo, standing at the top of the Leaning Tower, about to start his experiment by letting go of a ball. To be sure, that experiment was not an experiment at all but a demonstration of a remarkable fact already known by Galileo, namely that balls of different weights would, absent friction, hit the ground at the same time. That's somewhat to my point, since so-called information gathered by experimental research is, I would guess, far less often put to use as the source of new discoveries than as the corroboration of preconceived knowledge.

What is a little off my point is the mind-boggling and modernity-determining way in which Galileo proves the law on the basis of a postulate suggested by the Pisan demonstration. The postulate says that, since weight is not involved in free fall close to the earth's surface, the simplest possible relation of velocity to time is to be assumed, namely that the former varies directly with the latter. Then the velocity lines, set up horizontally on each moment of time, increase proportionally with the time of falling and so assume the outline of a trian-

---

[1] On the third day of Creation, the earth appears (*Gen.* 1:9).

gle whose base represents the velocity at the moment of impact. The interior of this triangle is a kind of proto-integral, a summation of all the near-infinitesimal velocity lines, with side t for time and d/t for distance per time, or velocity. These sides, when multiplied, yield twice the area of a triangle representing the dimension $t \times d/t = d$. Simply put, the *area* of a triangle, a plane figure, now represents a *distance*, a linear figure. I'm moved to say that this counterintuitive procedure instantiates the crucial effect of quantification: the symbolic quantity has no immediately apprehensible similarity to the quality of the symbolized phenomenon, here distance.

I must interrupt my account to say, very emphatically, that Galileo clearly saw what was eventuating and did his clever and careful best to circumvent the representation of distance by area, so that his proof is conceptually clean but mathematically cumbrous. More efficient but less mindful ways would soon be found.[2]

As it turns out, the tsunami of information currently available is largely numerical in form and bears a ruptured relation to its qualitative subject. Incidentally, the law of free fall then simply stares at you from the diagram—since by the postulate the velocity ratios are the same as the time ratios, we can substitute the time for the velocity and say: In free fall on earth, in abstraction from friction and in the absence of a force that might increase acceleration, the distances vary as the squares of the times, $d \sim t^2$. Let me repeat: I'm a little off topic with this tale, but only a little, since the story of non-similar symbolism is inextricably implicated in the tale of depth vs. complexity.

By recalling a moment when time went diagrammatically downward rather than outward I intend to remind you of other ways time goes downward—and *inward*. If Galileo's ball hadn't been stopped at the ground, it would, with time, have gone inward toward the center of the earth.

---

[2]In fact, this transmogrification had already preceded, when a *length* uniformly increasing had been made to symbolize a similarly increasing *rate*, namely the ratio of distance to time, or *velocity*.

There is another discipline with which I am familiar in which time heads down. In archaeology, the deeper we dug (I say "we" because in my pre-Socratic days I was an archeologist) and the later it drew in our personal day, the earlier it became in the world's time: the deeper down, the farther back. On Earth, the buried *past* lies progressively deeper below the visible *now* that presents itself on the surface. These material survivals went, if undisturbed, in readable stratifications, way back into prehistoric times.[3]

I refer to digging because it is an analogue, perhaps even *the* source of metaphor, for a psychic capacity called remembering. In *remembering* we dive into our memory tank, often to meet a memory floating or flashing up to forestall or even anticipate our search. But sometimes we must *recollect,* dig laboriously downward through stratum after stratum of compacted memories, until the one we seek halts the search. Socrates distinguishes memory (*mneme*) from recollection (*anamnesis*), (*e.g., Symposium* 208 A; *Meno* 81 D). Augustine, that great Platonic theologian, devises an imaginative topology of the soul which visualizes that depth-sounding destination of recollection (*Confessions,* Bk. X, Chs. 11, 12, 17). Our quasi-sensory memory images densely fill the innumerable fields and caves and caverns of our inward quasi-spatial memory. Here we wander in remembrance. Deeper yet within the huge inner world are placeless places for imageless presences such as true mathematical figures (meaning those drawn with *breadthless* lengths on an inner quasi-plane); precepts of the liberal arts, including logic; and the invisible being of things discerned within, "themselves by themselves," the Platonic forms. These flee into the remotest recesses and must be "excogitated," literally "driven to-

---

[3] "*If* undisturbed": I recall a day of excitement at the American Excavations of the Athenian Agora (Marketplace), when a pristine Neolithic deposit was thought to have been discovered. By evening the excavators had reached bottom—and there lay a little button bearing the legend: ARMY OF THE HELLENES. It came from a Greek army tunic; its presence spoiled the temporal virginity of the find and with it much of its informational value.

gether and out," in other words, laboriously recollected. Then Augustine extends the depth—or height—of the soul beyond memory and its recollective recesses: "I will transcend" (*transibo*), he says, my memory and "ascending" (*ascendans*) through and beyond my memorial soul I will mount up to God who is above me.

To my mind, this is a remarkable correction, or perhaps a consummation, of Socrates' account, who never tells, except in his post-mortem myths, how the forms and their ruling principle, the Idea of the Good, actually come into the soul—or it to them. In Augustine's account, they penetrate, they enter, the innermost depth of the soul, that is to say, the soul opens onto the heights of Heaven. Depth and height are strangely identical. I will dwell on this later, but for now I'll recall to you that the Latin word *altus* means both "high" and "deep," and also that Heraclitus says, "The way up and down is one and the same" (Fr. D-K 60).

Like Augustine, the enhancer of Platonic psychology, Freud, its traducer, sees an outside-in psychic topology. He himself called psychoanalysis "depth-psychology" (*Encyclopedia Britannica*, 1926). His early typology in the *Interpretation of Dreams* (1900) names at the upper end the perceptual system, that is, sensual awareness; behind or below comes the preconscious system, that is, the subconscious, where reside psychic facts not presently in awareness but readily accessible; and deep down is the place of the unconscious, a hermetic hell, reachable only by the experts in deep penetration, the psychoanalysts. The motto of Freud's early book is "If I cannot bend heaven, I will raise hell" (Virgil, *Aeneid* VII 312). And that is why I call Freud a traducer of the two ancients: For them, the light increases with depth; for him, the murk. As Lady Macbeth, who might, poor woman, be a Freudian case, says, "Hell is murky" (*Macbeth*, V i).

Let me return to Augustine's *Confessions*, Book XI (23, 27, 28), to my mind the high point of the inquiry into time. Here memory becomes the place and the condition of time. Time is a "distention" of the mind, a dilation brought about by its accumulating memories, and the amount of this mental stretching is the measure of times. Neither future nor past *is*; only the present, the here and now, *exists*. The future is expectation now and the past is memory now, and time is the presently felt extent of this expectational and memorial stretching upward into the future and downward into the past respectively.

To be sure, Augustine says nothing about up or down. But Husserl, who takes his departure from Augustine in what is probably the greatest application of the phenomenological method to a subject, his *Phenomenology of Internal Time-Consciousness* (1905), does exactly that in describing his own "Diagram of Time" (para. 10). He speaks of the new nows changing into pasts that continuously "run off' and plunge "downward" into the depths marked on a vertical line which symbolizes the "retention," that is to say, the memory of impressions.

To complete all these preliminaries, let me take a minute to tell you about the etymologies of the words "deep" and "down." I am far from imagining that recovered meanings, be they the careful etymologies produced by learned linguists, who trace a word to its speculative Indo-European root, or the creative derivations devised by imaginative amateurs, which have no basis in research, prove anything at all. The dead-serious but linguistically dubious etymologizing of certain philosophers strikes me as an improbity, while the apt hijinks of others seem to me good fun.[4] But both linguistically sound etymologies and imaginative verbal *jeux d'esprit* can be thought-provoking, the

---

[4]An example of—how shall I put it?—unstraightforwardness is Heidegger's translation of Greek *aletheia*, "truth," as "un-concealedness," as from alpha-privative *a* ("un") and *lethe* ("forgetfulness"), from a verb that means "to elude notice." The etymology has some support, but there is no evidence that to early and classical authors *aletheia* meant anything but truth and genuineness as opposed to falseness and counterfeit. An example of fun is from Plato's *Phaedrus* (252 C): *Pteros* means "Winged Eros," since *pteron* means "feather."

Again from the *Phaedrus* (e.g., 234 C), the joining of words for love and loving, question and questioning, which sound alike in Greek, is suggestive wordplay. The *Symposium* is also full of this pun. (Some puns are, after all, covert etymological claims.) And above all, the *Cratylus* is one long etymological extravagance.

latter because they're *meant* to be, the former because they *may* tell us something about the development of human reflection. But all in all, etymologies are incitements, not revelations, and poetic play, not philosophy.

Here is the linguistically respectable etymology of "deep." The Indo-European root *dheub* gives rise to "dip," "dive," as well as "deep." Thus it is reasonable to infer that "deep" originally signified plunging into an element and bringing up some of it. The deepest dipping and diving our earth affords is the ocean, the deepest of the deep, the Mariana Trench; let it stand for non-metaphorical, literal, depth and diving. The "down" adjective is similarly physical; it derives from *dune*, "hill"; "down" means "off the hill," moving from top to bottom.

Now let me do the same for "complexity." "Com-," Indo-European *kom*, signifies "beside, near, with"; "-plexity" derives from *plek-*, "to plait," originally from "flax," a plant yielding textile fiber. So like depth, complexity is rooted in our dealing with material objects. I've read that the most complicated object known to us is our brain. I don't need to insist that its complexity is non-metaphorical, literal, just because I believe that complexity hardly ever *is* a metaphor.

We deal with complexity by *"ex-*plicating," that is, undoing the *im-*plicating entanglements of complexity, or by "ex-plaining," that is, setting complexities out plainly. The two meanings of the word "plain," that is, "clear" and "flat," have the same origin: the wide "plain" is where things are plain because the view is unobstructed, and the mathematical flat surface, the "plane," has the same origin. Hence "explaining" is a mode of extracting meaning that explicates its subject by projecting it onto a flat surface. Thus, for instance, the brain is contained by a roughly round skull (because, I imagine, the sphere is that mathematical solid which has the lowest ratio of surface to content), so that its involutions need to be explicated in plane surfaces: in marked cross sections for viewing and labeled schemata for functions and plane mappings for neural networks.

What I've just said can serve to deal with an annoying sort

of argumentative deflection. Someone will interject, to derail you: "It's more complex than that." To which the answer is: "Well then, if you mean it, draw me a picture." For complexity is *the* eminently diagrammable, spatializable problem; it can be set out plainly. To be sure, complexity is the opposite of simplicity, and what these folks often say as the final put-down is: "You're being simplistic. You're over-simplifying." To which the apparently merely *eristic*, that is, contentious, answer is: "And you're being shallow, superficial," meaning: your overview has too few nodes and connections to begin with and doesn't go *into* the matter to boot.

Now to the point of my talk: to show, perhaps a little too briefly, that it is not merely critical to say that complexity is a superficial view of the world, but also has real non-derogatory meaning, and then to conclude by attempting a description and—I'll be upfront about it—a defense of depth. Just as I don't want to say that they are opposite kinds of thinking, far be it from me to claim that complexity and depth are "kinds" of thinking at all. To my mind, it is plain unthinking to claim that there are different ways of thinking. Thinking is always thinking—always the same in being "about" something, thus always qualified by what it is about. It is always the same but often *about* something different. For, of course, there are different *objects* of thought, different ways to see what you must think about.[5] Thus the people who used to be referred to as primitives, and before that as savages, felt surrounded by well- or ill-intentioned spirits and, most rationally, concluded that they needed to propitiate these spirits in ways they themselves might respond to—just as we would.

Or take Socrates. Some folks say that he was interested in defining certain objects, that is, in delimiting them in the universe of discourse, in explaining them and their interrelations

---

[5] People also employ different devices, modes, ways of thinking, such as figures, analogies, conjectures; it is hard to see how they could do it, except against a backdrop of plain mentation.

verbally. Well, so he was, but only when they were heavily affected with non-being, as in his multi-definitional pursuit of the sophist in the dialogue of that name, the results of which I've spent some amusing hours diagramming. But when he is within view of a true being—one of the human excellences, for example—asking that notorious "What is . . . ?" question, his aim is *not* definition, but a delving descent to depths attained in literal "under-standing" (as we say) or in a truth-following ascent to the heights achieved through "over-standing" or *episteme* (as the Greeks say). It is always thinking, but sometimes of words, or about objects, or from different positions. Consider that if thinking weren't always just that we wouldn't even know we have thoughts different from someone else's.

Now to some gist. What *is* complexity? Well, first, there are several kinds I've discerned and no doubt others I haven't.

There's Wittgenstein's kind, very clearly set out in the *Philosophical Investigations* (Part I, 1945, Part II, 1949). He says at one point: "The *deep* aspect eludes us easily" (I 387, 594). "Do not try to analyze the experience *in* yourself" (II xi, my italics). So we are to turn to the public use of words, for example, explanations (I 69) and the behavior it induces, called the "language game."[6] The external view, he says, "reveals a complicated network of similarities overlapping and criss-crossing" (I 66). His figure here appears to be one-dimensional, a thread of overlapping fibers (I 67), but since these also criss-cross, the real figure is clearly two- or three-dimensional. This is *verbal* complexity, and it is characterized by *overtness, extensive relational-*

---

[6] It seems to me that the language game, which teaches meaning by ostension, doesn't work except for a dull-witted apprentice: Master teaches pupil the word "slab" (flagstone) by pointing to an exemplar and then sends him to fetch another from a pile (I 6). If he's dull enough, he'll come back with a slab, but if he's brightly observant, he'll come back and say: "I didn't see another just like this one." The master will be thrown back on communicating *The Slab*, itself by itself, since no one, I think, can see likeness except through modeling essence— but the last clause goes beyond my present point, which is not to advocate *a* philosophy, but a way of inquiry. (In my heart I believe that it is likely to lead to certain realizations, for example, that some entities have essences or that there is being which transcends perception.)

ity, and *interconnectivity*: "family resemblances" (*ibid*.); its point is to get on with practicalities; speech is known from its use in the world.

Another kind of complexity can be characterized as *computable*: It has sharply defined digital elements related by rules of computation, that is, problem-solving procedures, algorithms. This complexity is hard-edged: digits in clear calculational relations. The point is to get the solution to the kind of pre-formulated question called a "problem," whose relation to human experience is determined by the fiat of postulation.

Yet a third kind of complexity is *informational*, characterizable as bits of fact, raw or inferred, singular or aggregated in categories. Information has only *relative* existence; in its first nature it is like a mud flat, which becomes discrete only when handfuls are molded into a clump of clay. Abstract information is therefore irrelevantly pre-formed pseudo-knowledge. Thus information, even when verifiable, consists of relational factoids that become active facts in a context of human intention. Information becomes relevant to final decision-making when a desire is formulated and an intention is formed. Then the point is usually to underwrite the desired action, or to modify, even to cancel it, if the facts are really terminally unspinnable.

My final, but surely not last, kind of complexity is psychical and social—that is, human. I won't attempt to delineate it. Its elements are too various in kind and degree and their relations too difficult, be it by human intention or natural obscurity. Ungifted experts tend to deliver very gross conceptual depictions of the human world, but very great psychologists and anthropologists (the latter need to be the former more than the converse, I think) manage to combine an extensive overview with penetrating insight. I am thinking of the Greeks' Herodotus and our Tocqueville. They manage to survey the many interrelated phenomena that surface on our earth and to clue out underlying, I would say, *the* underlying distinctions and commonalities.

Here, by a natural and easy transition (as Robert Brum-baugh used to say, when he meant quite a leap[7]), I shall try to speak of depth. It might seem presumptuous, did I not think that one may speak of it without having been there: *Trying is all.*

To begin with, the deep divers that I have read and even known display respect for and acquaintance with phenomenal complexities.[8] I say "phenomenal" because the juxtaposition of *phainomena* and *onta*, sensed "appearances" and intellected "be-ings," must surely underlie the distinction between complex-ity and depth. Let me here say again that complexity usually is and means to be a literal description of its realm, while depth is a metaphor, a figural application of a this-worldly phenome-non: dipping and diving into a material element.[9]

Thereby hangs a tale, a tale I will foretell in a sentence: There is *no*, repeat, *no* way of speaking of the soul and of the realm whose emissary it is except by analogy (prosaically) or by metaphor (poetically). Indeed, all philosophical speech is, I dare to claim, figurative. Let me remind you of two prime ex-amples. Plato's Socrates speaks of *eidos*, literally "look" or "as-pect." But the word is used "meta-phorically," which means "carried over" into the realm of thought, in which reside the beings that have "invisible looks." (Mythically and punningly their place is in the underwold: *Aides aeides*, "Hades the Invisi-ble,"[10] *Phaedo* 80 D, *Cratylus* 404 B.[11]) Or take the Stoic invention

---

[7] At Yale, I slipped in and out (more out) of his lectures, the only graduate class in philosophy I ever attended at all. The required undergraduate course at Brook-lyn College was a big nothing.

[8] "Even known": Jacob Klein, Dean of St. John's College when I arrived there in 1957.

[9] Thus descriptions that mean to delve are usually simplifications. Of whom is it truer to say "you're simplifying" than of a novelist who is experienced in delin-eating the soul and the world? By "simplifying" I mean the writer's ability to penetrate a complex character by a descriptive detail, to reach deep into the soul with a single word.

[10] *Aeides*: an allusion to the un-murky Greek Hades (*Aides*), the underworld where dwell luminously invisible things.

[11] In other dialogues they are located up high (*Symposium* 211), in the heavens (*Phaedrus* 247).

of the "concept," literally a "grasping together [of particulars]."
These metaphorical ways, the poetry of philosophy, are not, to
my mind, primitive evidence of some logic-overleaping access
to the Unconcealed that hides itself from the prosaic professors,
but our one possible way to reach beyond the sensory world by
taking advantage of the *deadness* of the metaphors that make up
our latter-day language. It is a semi-extinction that allows us to
use our words *as if* they had always meant what we mean them
to mean: non-sensory beings directly denoted by pure imageless speech. Who hears "concept" as an assembling grasp, or
"logic" as a collecting art?[12]

So dead metaphors are a means of conning ourselves into
believing that we have direct access to supersensory realms.
But bringing them alive is a way to candid confrontation with
transcendence.

To be sure, Aristotle and Wittgenstein actually agree—
imagine this!—that there is articulable thinking not in need
of quasi-sensory imagining. For Aristotle it is the highest kind
that functions without imagination: intellecting, *noesis*, the direct apprehension of the knowable. For Wittgenstein no understanding of a proposition is in need of imagining (*On the Soul*
1129a ff.; *Philosophical Investigation* I 396). I can believe it of Aristotle that *his* mind, his *nous*, had such a capacity for viewless
thinking, sightless insight—do any of ours?[13]

So, I claim, whether or not we are practicing etymologists,
whether we are literally the "truth-tellers" about our first words
(for that is the etymology of "etymology"), their defunct spirits
tug at us to return to them.

No way to speak of underlying being non-somatically, I said
a moment ago, and no way to go into sightless depths (divers
without goggles do keep their eyes closed) without first taking
in the surface, the place of laid-out overtness, of infinite par-

---

[12] Logic: from Greek *logos*; the root is *leg-*, as in "collect."

[13] It is practically undecidable whether either Socrates or Plato ever claimed to
have come within intellectual sight of the forms.

ticularity, of connecting context. Here's another Socratic corroboration: Socrates is generally and inattentively presented
as denigrating the multifarious and shifting phenomenal surface on which we crawl about. But I already mentioned that
he, an inveterate urbanite, who says that country places don't
teach him a thing, had more local knowledge and more sce-
nic sensibility than his companion, a suburban stroller. And in
the *Symposium* (206 B ff.), Socrates, we learn, has been taught by
his mentor, Diotima, to think that the ascent into the heights
of being must start with the surely complex, and mostly sur-
face-captivated, experience of falling in love, which is also the
first glimpse into psychic depths. The same is true of Aristotle and Thomas and Hegel, who all seem to know a lot about
worldly and human complexity, especially the monk.[14] I'm not
just dropping names here but citing concrete examples of experiential expansiveness.

Having given complexity its due, what then *is* depth, this
mode figuratively orthogonal to complexity, a mode more *askew
of* than *opposite to* it? But I will stall one last time: What is depth
and the way down *not*?

1. It cannot, by its very nature, be governed by the formalisms of logic. For it is always reached through the revealing veil
of metaphor, which assures that the blunt first law of logic be set
aside, the one that proscribes "p · ~ p." This law of non-contradiction forbids that a proposition be at once true and not true,
though for its first formulator, Aristotle, this is not a formal

---

[14] Thomas: His "Treatise on the Passions" in the *Summa Theologiae* seems to me
unsurpassable; consider also Aristotle's researches in the animal kingdom and
Hegel on history and the arts.

The last page of Hegel's *Phenomenology of the Spirit* speaks pretty nearly
exactly in my terms, depth vs. complexity, only in the opposite direction. Here
the realm of Spirit, of inwardness, undergoes a sequence of revelations in which
its "depth" (*Tiefe*) is superseded by an "externalization" or alienation (*Entäusse-
rung*), whose aim is the "revelation of depth," by an "extension" (*Ausdehnung*) in
space of the inwardly-centered ego, which is the "I being itself" (*sichselbstseiendes
Ich*). It is a revelation that effects the "saving cancellation" (*Aufhebung*) of this
depth. Hegel is speaking of the time-delivered incarnation of God on earth; I
am thinking only of the atemporal withdrawal of human beings from the world.

axiom but an affirmation that its intentional object, the thing meant in declaratory speech, is always a determinate being, which either is or is not. So with acquiescence in the law of thinking and being goes this very implication, that the spatial world is determinately, positively, what it is. Not so the depths. The way down is very much a *via negativa* on the one hand: "I don't really mean what my speech is saying"—and *therefore*, on the other, a *via in-ventionis*, a way of "going into," of discovery— of things not quite thinkable, yet somehow divined.

2. Nor is depth-diving a way of *deduction*, of the logical descent from maxims to conclusion, nor of *induction*, the logical ascent from facts to generalizations, for these procedures can be plainly laid out.

3. Nor are the depths a mere *alternative universe* of discourse, an idly eccentric language game, since, I am convinced, urgent intimations from that quarter, from our internality, those pulls that *precede* articulated speech, are a common, an ineluctable, human experience. This is a claim scarcely capable of verification other than by testimonial. But I simply believe that even people who revel in their own and their world's brutely overt materiality are visited by such transcendent innuendos.

4. Nor is the way into depths subject to a Cartesian *method*, prescribed by teachable *rules for the direction of the mind*,[15] since thinking, willing to be methodical in its articulated stretches, is *open*, receptive rather than constraining.

WHAT THEN, FINALLY, is depth and the way down?

To begin with, Heraclitus says: "The way up and down is one and the same" (D-K 60).[16] I'll adapt that to my purpose.

[15] Descartes, *Discourse on Method* (1637), *Rules for the Direction of the Mind* (1628).

[16] He might concede that *my* experience of the way up and back is different, because I'm facing in opposite directions, but still, the overseeing Logos will give the same account of both. For the Heraclitean Logos is both immanent, as determining the ratios (*logoi*) of the elemental transformations of nature, and transcendent, as the one who gathers, collects (*legei*) Everything into One; it is the latter Logos who contracts up and down into one.

Perhaps I can put it thus: The way of our search and its discoveries leads deep down into the depths of our soul or mind
or consciousness toward what is found *last* but *is* in itself *first*,
a grounding finality.[17] Once discovered, it becomes the ruling principle (*arche*) of our account-giving as we come back up
onto earth. So the delving and climbing reach the same end, an
"alpha and omega," the immediate insight *and* its articulated
expression.

That is the *way*, but the *mode* of our search is question-asking rather than problem-solving. In this phraseology, depth is
the venue of *questions*, complexity, of *problems*. Statements of
problems can actually do without question-marks; they are *perplexities* presented to be explicated, straightened out, conceptually or practically. Or, if you like, a problem is a hard-edged,
well-defined question with a correspondingly jigged answer
drawn from a predetermined pool of possibilities.

For example, here's a metaphysical problem: to discern the
number of causes operative in the world. The solution is constrained by such presumptions as these: Everything this-
worldly has a cause, including apparent chance (Aristotle,
Physics Bk. II iv ff.); therefore, if anything is uncaused or self-
caused it is a divinity (*ibid.*, Bk. VIII, *Metaphysics*, Bk. XII).
Causes are multiple because the world is complexly constituted. And they are "responsible," meaning that they come to
us as responses forced from the beings pinned down by an in-
terrogation. And so forth. The solution is definite, and the dis-
cussion continues only insofar as some people reject it.

Here's a practical problem: On my way back from Athens,
it'll be a problem how to navigate the notoriously long security
lines of your Atlanta airport. When I get to the front, I'll think

---

[17]My version of Aristotle, *Physics* (184 a): "The way is from things more knowable to us and clearer, to things clearer by nature and more knowable." There is
another meaning of "ground," not mine here. It is the *a priori*, the conceptually
prior basement upon which to construct an epistemological edifice, an explana-
tory system such as Kant erects (*Critique of Pure Reason*, B 860).

of other things. Solving practical problems takes this-worldly know-how; solving philosophical problems takes other-worldly activity. In either case, when a problem is really *solved*, it is also *dissolved*; it becomes moot. People preoccupied by solved problems are told to get a life. (There actually are some solved philosophical problems that stay solved, mostly those involving a superseded physics.[18])

Questions, on the other hand, seem to me not properly perplexities. They don't go away—they are perennial—not because they are demonstrably insoluble but because they are not proposed for solving but rather for going into, deeper and deeper.

The *mode* of engagement with questions, as I delineate it for myself, is what Socrates calls *aporia*, literally waylessness.[19] Therefore the way of searching out the deep is indeed a *methodos*, a "way-to-be-followed," but only in the sense of an oriented movement, not in the modern meaning of a *method*, a progress guided by procedures.

Entertaining questions thus requires *wisdom*, a considering, reflecting frame of a mind still resonating with past experience but now focused by desirous expectation. Otherwise put: Questions are a mode of *blessed ignorance*, a thorough apprehen-

[18]Some of these do in fact remain interesting, sometimes as testimonials to the concrete impasses that make grand theories implode.

[19]Or "unprovidedness." The above meditation on modes of searching has as a background Book III of Aristotle's *Metaphysics*, which marks the transition of philosophy from amateur *question-asking* to professional *problem-solving*, the second such transition in the West. The first was from pre-Socratic *initiation* into Logos or Truth by a divinity to the Socratic *search* by going into oneself.

The word "problem" is not actually used by Aristotle in Book III; in fact he speaks of "difficulties" and *aporiai*, which I think he assimilates to "problems" in our sense. Plato already uses *problema* in the geometry-derived sense. A problem asks for a construction, which yields a product, as opposed to a theorem, which gives insight. Some ancients—this is to my point—objected to the notion of a mathematical problem, since mathematics is about knowing, not making (Heath, *Euclid's Elements*, I 125). By this distinction hangs a tale extending into modernity, but beyond the scope of this talk: the development of mathematical objects from concrete items to abstracted symbols.

sion of our own cognitive limitations, which clears our minds of mere opinions and, while it prevents us from reaching for personal originality rather than objective origins, moves us inward.[20]

A question, then, is a receptive opening in us—who knows in what capacity of ours. The reception is expectant of an answer—of a spontaneous intimation rather than a driven determination, of an incitement more than a settlement, of a mental vision or a verbal hypothesis instead of a conclusive solution. Such responses are often fraught simplicities, not abrogations of difficulties but rather problem-generating fecundities.[21]

The *aim* of asking questions is to penetrate spatio-temporal experience so as to reach the atemporal inwardness, com-

---

[20] "Blessed ignorance" is my adaptation of Nicolas of Cusa's title *Of Learned Ignorance* (*De Docta Ignorantia*, 1440)—"blessed" for "learned" because, of course, it's precisely *not* learned, that is, schooled. Even though lots of graduates might be correctly awarded an I.D., an *Ignorantiae Doctor*, it would be in the wrong spirit. What Cusanus means by learned ignorance is the fully realized desire to know that has become unobstructed when we have thoroughly learned our ignorance (Bk. I i). Directing features of this desire are the *via negativa* (the way of gaining a foothold in the transcendent by what it is not), *conjecture* (the way of holding a well-motivated opinion firmly enough to go on with but flexibly enough for alteration), and *analogy* (the way of levering up thought by recognizing similarities in different venues and through these likenesses discovering differences). I think that these ways are mutually implicated, but I have neither studied Cusanus enough nor sufficiently thought out my notions.

[21] Prime examples are to be found in the sayings of Heraclitus and Parmenides, the two pre-Socratics distinguished by being not "physical" (Aristotle, *Physics* 186 b), but meta-physical. Here is one example. Parmenides says: "For it is the same both to be aware (*noein*) and to be" (Fr. D-K 3; Fr. D-K 8, line 34)—most often translated along these lines: "For the same thing can be thought as can be." Heidegger interprets ingeniously in line with his notion of unconcealment: Being's essence *involves* being apprehended (*Introduction to Metaphysics*, 1935 [106]).

I think we should not subvert bold depth by refusing to read what is written. Parmenides regards Being as One, for which his figure is a sphere. So he countermands the multiplicity inherent in his spherical metaphor by gnomically intimating that Being is self-aware, self-translucent, self-implicated—as unextended, partless, undifferentiable, being everywhere and nowhere, just as is awareness when its object is itself.

monly called the essence, whose surface is the appearance. Here I should stop because I am allowing myself to be carried away toward an ontological speculation from what I would be glad to call merely a meditation on, or at most a phenomenology of, inquiry.[22]

ARE THERE CONSEQUENCES TO the preceding exposition? To my mind, there are personal ones, surely—such as the acquisition of a template to gauge what you're doing and to judge if a quarter turn inside and down might be desirable. There are disciplinary ones, probably—such as querying cognitive scientists about the feasibility of inward-turned mental depth emerging from that ultimate complex structure, the brain. And there are institutional ones, possibly—such as a reconsideration by philosophy departments of their highest degree, now the Ph.D., *Philosophiae Doctor*. It is, after all, a comical title, which claims that you are a proficient preceptor, a *doctor*, of the love of wisdom, a teacher, that is, of love—a situation nowadays full of moral and legal pitfalls. Departments might add a secondary and more sensible degree, the Ph.D.$_2$, to be read as *Philosophiae Dilector*, a "delighter and dilettante in the love of wisdom," to be awarded to elicitors rather than preceptors of philosophy. For I think that while the *mapping of complexity*, which is an institutional way of "doing" philosophy, can keep people promotion-worthily busy and often contentedly absorbed, the *dilettantish delvers into depths*, the future inciters rather than professors, amateurish because philosophy true to its name cannot be a profession, might also have their diploma,

---

[22]I regard it as somewhat corroborative of the descriptive verity of my depth metaphor for a tendency of inquiry that it plays no discernible role for Heidegger either in *Being and Time* (1927), where *phainomena* and *onta* are assimilated [31, 35], or in the *Introduction to Metaphysics*, where Being is self-emergent and involves its own manifesting appearance as a defining delimitation [77]. The reason for this absence is, I think, that *Dasein* (an abstraction from a *human being*) which *is* only in caring about its being, is altogether temporal and this-worldly—so perforce a-metaphorical and un-deep.

though such diving may bring up nothing much but deep delight:

> Could I revive within me
> Her symphony and song,
> To such a deep delight t'would win me . . .
>   —Coleridge, "Kubla Khan"